MAKING M
—FROM—
YOUR HOME

MAKING MONEY
—FROM—
YOUR HOME

Over 100 ways
to earn extra income

HAZEL EVANS

PIATKUS

© 1994 Hazel Evans

First published in 1994 by
Judy Piatkus (Publishers) Ltd
5 Windmill Street, London W1P 1HF

**The moral right of the author
has been asserted**

*A catalogue record for this book is available
from the British Library*

ISBN 0-7499-1360-6

Designed by Chris Warner

Set in Linotron Sabon by
Create Publishing Services, Bath
Printed & bound in Great Britain by
Biddles Ltd, Guildford & King's Lynn

Contents

Introduction   7

Section One: Deciding what's your line
   and getting started   13

Section Two: Making your house work for you   30

Section Three: Cooking from home   48

Section Four: Business ideas   74

Section Five: Using your skills: Arts and Crafts   102

Section Six: Green-finger ideas   134

Section Seven: Working with people and
   animals   155

Section Eight: The Help section   178

Index   202

For John

Introduction

IT'S AN ALL TOO FAMILIAR scene these days: your house suddenly seems to have become a burden. Maybe it's too big: the children have gone out into the world and now you've all that room to spare. But you're reluctant to leave because, after all, it's the family home. Perhaps, on the other hand, you traded up and bought something more ambitious – and now are caught in a money trap with an over-large mortgage and unsaleable property. You could be stuck with the house for another reason: the loss of a partner, or the loss of your job.

Look at the situation in a positive way: a house is a potential asset in your life, one in which you have invested a great deal, and could now exploit to bring in valuable cash. You can do this in two ways: by making the building itself earn its keep, or by using it as your workplace, the springboard from which to start up an entirely new career.

So, if you like the idea of having some extra money, if you're looking for a new interest or even a new lifestyle that will not cost you a great deal of capital, then think in terms of cashing in on your house in some way.

As an impassioned house-owner I know what it is to be in that sort of situation. Several years ago I fell in love with a big old bastide in a village in Provence. I took out a second mortgage and bought it. After two years of expensive conversion work I ended up with more rooms than I needed – and bills to match. So I decided to make the house work for its keep, and have an excuse to stay there more often. I began running holidays in midsummer for people who wanted to write or paint, and it prospered beyond my wildest dreams. It is now a successful arts centre run by my daughter and son-in-law, which is full all summer, so I've had to move out and buy another house to live in!

It could be, of course, that you have no need – or desire – to sell your house. Your motivation for reading this book might be rather that you wish to exploit the money-making potential of a large garden. It could be that you have just retired and have time on your hands. Or you could be one of the thousands each year who tire of the nine to five run, or have been unexpectedly made redundant, and are thinking of setting up business from home on their own. Or perhaps you're unable to go out to work on a formal basis because of a growing family or dependent relatives but need something stimulating to do.

Whatever the reason, you'll find this book can help. All the ideas it contains can be taken up in a small way and expanded at your own pace. And they are all written up from practical experience, for I've started more than twenty businesses from home in my time, ranging from a dogs' model agency to a vineyard, so I know what I'm talking about. What happened to my businesses? I'm proud to say that not one foundered. I simply sold them on, and started something else!

SEIZING THE MOMENT

Times of recession, strangely enough, can be a good time to set up a small business if – and here is the important point – **if** you do not have to risk your capital or borrow large sums of money to make a start. In previous times when the economic climate was bad, many people turned a hobby into a successful enterprise. The famous Ryder Cup, renowned throughout the golfing world, is named after a certain Mr Ryder who began to save and sell seeds from his back garden in the midst of a recession in the 1920s. Starting from home he built up a business worth millions – and was able to indulge his passion for golf as a result.

Despite the state of the economy, bear in mind that there *are* people around out there with money to spend – particularly on something they really covet. And it's possible that **you** could be the person to supply that very thing. You may not make an instant fortune, but your enterprise might well pay for your family holiday in its first year. And you can slowly and steadily build up to a good income.

Retired?

The age of retirement, just when most people are thinking of winding down, is in many ways the best time to start working for yourself; particularly if you are being dragged, screaming and kicking, into a life of inactivity. You've got the safety net of a pension, however small it may be, and provided that your idea does not involve laying out precious capital, or eating into your pension fund, you have the time to devote to something new. If you are not desperate for money, you can start in a small way and gradually build up a business.

Redundant?

If you've been made redundant and despaired of getting another job, starting up one of your own may entitle you to money or training via official loans, government training or business expansion schemes. At the time of publication, many small entrepreneurs are being helped in the early stages with some basic funding, but the situation is so volatile that it is impossible to give totally up-to-date guide-lines. However, the Help Section at the back of this book will give you suggestions, and names and addresses of individuals and organisations able to help you find out what's available.

In both the case of retirement and redundancy, circumstances have made it impossible for you to go on with your job, but you have one big plus: you're bound to have acquired a back-log of practical experience of some kind. In short, you've 'been there, seen that, done that'.

Lonely?

Working from home can be a great antidote to boredom or unhappiness, for it gives your life a sense of purpose. It can be a great way to make friends, too. Many of the more gregarious ways of working at or from home, with the local contacts they give, can be a good way to meet new people. If you have been feeling isolated up to now, it gives you a chance to become part of the community. Above all, making money for yourself gives you independence and self-confidence – makes you feel more self-sufficient. These very qualities, strangely enough, make you a much more interesting and attractive proposition to other people. It's at this stage, very often, that you start to make new friends.

No more commuting...

There's nothing new about working from home. In centuries gone by it was the norm. But the industrial revolution put paid to all that, uprooting people from their homes, drawing them into the big cities. Now, in the 1990s, there's a swing back towards home-based activities. It is predicted that, thanks to technology such as the fax, the phone, and the computer, many people who commute to factories and offices today will be doing the same job from home in the near future. After all, it is even possible to hold in-depth discussion without the people concerned actually meeting, thanks to 'talk-in' phone lines. And soon we'll be able to see each other too, via video screens.

Think of all the advantages there are to home-based work. You don't have the expense, and wear and tear, of travelling back and forth, saving on money, time and temper. And you probably don't have to put on special clothes – you can work all day, if you like, in a track suit or shorts and running shoes rather than a tailored suit.

You can also start and stop when you like. You're free, you have no one to answer to, no 9 to 5 regime. You can make your own hours, building them around family and friends. As your own boss, you make the choices. And you don't necessarily need special training – your skills as a householder may well be more than adequate.

HOW TO USE THIS BOOK

You may already know exactly how and in what capacity you want to work from home, or you may be toying with several different ideas – you may even have a completely open mind. To get the best out of this book, first fill in the questionnaire in Section One. This will force you to think carefully about your project and decide your fitness to carry it out.

Then turn to the section that most interests you and, having read that, if you want to take things further, turn to the Help Section at the back which lists further reading and the relevant organisations that may help. It also tells you all you need to know, at this stage, about marketing, accounting, company law and tax.

GO FOR IT!

Your name will not be added to the list of businesses that fail. Most of those needed heavy investment in stock or materials, and the negotiation of bank loans to fund such enterprise. Or they might have been providing a service that was no longer needed. In your case, you will investigate the market thoroughly, invest only what you can afford, and turn your money over quickly.

So go for it. You may need nothing more than a table and a telephone to begin with, or you may find yourself converting a spare room into a bed-sitter to bring in extra cash. Either way, you will have made a start!

Deciding What's Your Line and Getting Started

*Questionnaire ... What your score reveals ...
Some final, crucial questions ... Getting started ...
How to be a happy home-worker ... Your family,
help or hindrance ... Motivating yourself ... The
clothes you wear*

ASK YOURSELF before you rush headlong into any enterprise: 'Am I doing this because I sincerely want to?'

Your choice of job is important. Working on something you dislike, alone at home, can in many ways be worse than doing the same job in an office. Not least because there is no one to grumble to or with. It is vital that you **enjoy** what you are going to do. The answers you give to the following questionnaire will help you decide whether working at home would be appropriate for you, and if so, what sort of work would be most rewarding for someone of your particular disposition and circumstances.

QUESTIONNAIRE: DECIDING WHAT'S YOUR LINE

Answer yes or no to the following questions: score two points for a yes answer, one point for a no.

Set one

Yes No

☐ ☐ Do you make most of your friends via your work?
☐ ☐ Do you ever feel lonely?
☐ ☐ Do you like bouncing ideas off other people?
☐ ☐ Do you like working in a bustling atmosphere?
☐ ☐ If you're alone, do you listen to the radio a lot?
☐ ☐ Do you enjoy being one of a team?
☐ ☐ Do you like eating lunch out or at a canteen?
☐ ☐ Do you dislike your own company?
☐ ☐ Are you not quite sure what job you want to do?
☐ ☐ Do you dream of being rich?
☐ ☐ Are you fed up with commuting?
☐ ☐ Do you feel that you have been passed over for promotion?
☐ ☐ Do you hate the boss?
☐ ☐ Do you think you'll be able to relax more at home?
☐ ☐ Do you prefer not to take risks?

Set two

Yes No

☐ ☐ Do you chat to the doorman, and the telephonist at work, and to people in shops?
☐ ☐ Do you have plenty of energy?
☐ ☐ Are you good at persuading people to do things?
☐ ☐ Have you a naturally cheerful disposition?
☐ ☐ Do you know your neighbours well?
☐ ☐ Do you have a thriving social life?
☐ ☐ Could you be 'pushy' if you had to be?
☐ ☐ Are you seldom, if ever, embarrassed?
☐ ☐ Can you cope with difficult people?

Set three

Yes No

☐ ☐ Do you find it difficult to start work each morning?
☐ ☐ Does competition worry you?

Yes No
☐ ☐ Do you give in easily?
☐ ☐ Do you tend to let things get you down?
☐ ☐ Do you dislike change?
☐ ☐ Do you like to have someone to lean on, to solve problems for you?
☐ ☐ Do you prefer being at home to being at work?
☐ ☐ Do you dislike taking risks?
☐ ☐ Do you like being left to get on with a job without interference?
☐ ☐ Have you always felt that you were brighter than your superiors at work?
☐ ☐ Will you have to employ others to handle some aspects of your potential business?
☐ ☐ Are you security conscious?
☐ ☐ Do you like to stick to a routine?
☐ ☐ Are you basically rather shy?
☐ ☐ Do you want to get out of the rat race?

Set four

Yes No
☐ ☐ Do you have any capital at all to draw on?
☐ ☐ If you need financial help could you raise it?
☐ ☐ Are you on good terms with your Bank Manager?
☐ ☐ Do you have a pension?
☐ ☐ Do you know anything about income tax, VAT, national insurance?
☐ ☐ Could you start your business in your spare time now?
☐ ☐ Are you 'good' with money?

Set five

(Only relevant if you have a partner or a family)
Yes No
☐ ☐ Does your partner work, or are your family out most of the day?
☐ ☐ Have you told them about your ideas?
☐ ☐ Do they like the ideas?
☐ ☐ Would you like to bring your family into the business?

WHAT YOUR SCORE REVEALS

Set one

The lower your score is here, the more likely you are to be happy running a business from home, for you are self-sufficient enough to work on your own without feeling the need of a 'people fix'. You also don't feel the need to have other people involved.

If your score is between 22 and 30 you may not particularly enjoy your present job, but you should think carefully before giving it up at this stage. You obviously get most of your stimulation from a team-based atmosphere. If you do decide to work from home, make sure it is the type of job where you are in contact with other people all the time. Fortunately, there are plenty to choose from.

Set two

If your score is between 8 and 18 you are obviously a positive, outgoing person who could probably take rebuffs on the chin. Selling, in any shape or form is your metier, and you have enough resilience to be able to do it by yourself from home.

If you score 6 or less, this does not mean that you are not suited to working from home, but it does mean that you would be at your happiest providing a service of some sort, or making something, rather than doing a sales job. We all have to promote ourselves, or our product, but you would be happier leaving aggressive direct selling to someone else.

Set three

Score low, here, to be sure of business success. It's a tough world out there, and you need to have the know-how and the resilience to cope. The higher you score, the less successful you are likely to be at running a business.

If you rate 20 to 32, and you want to work at home, you would do better being employed as an outworker by someone else, or doing something creative-based, rather than having to run a structured business yourself.

Set four

Some businesses can be started on a shoe-string, but it's always best to have some sort of safety net. The higher the score the better, in this case, for you may have unexpected bills to meet. If you score less than 6, do not attempt to start a business that needs funding from the outset. It's far better to start small and grow gradually; even better if you can begin it in your spare time, while still in a job.

Set five

Starting a new career is challenging enough, but if you try to do it with no co-operation, even active hostility, from those around you, it can be very demoralising. Score only 5 or 4, and you should only work from home if it is something that won't impinge on family time, or you may be in difficulties.

Score 6 to 8, however, and it sounds as though the family are right behind you, and may even help you to make a success of it.

SOME FINAL, CRUCIAL QUESTIONS

Whatever your scores in the above questionnaire, the following questions, and your answers, will help you assess the job you're planning to do, and point up which areas you need to do further work on before attempting to put your idea into practice.

- What do you want to achieve?
- Do you have something worth selling?
- Is there any competition?
- How well are they doing?
- What sort of people live in your immediate neighbourhood?
- How big is your potential market?
- What do you already know about what you're planning to do?
- Do you need any training?
- Do you have the equipment you need?

- Are there any local by-laws, rules and regulations you should know about?

GETTING STARTED

Before you begin, check out what you can or can't do in the confines of your own home. If you have a mortgage, for instance, you may have to get the mortgager's permission to let all or part of it. Also, many homes have bizarre covenants on them. For example, although I own a flat in town with no ground, the lease states that I am not allowed to keep chickens. My sister, who has never had an ambition to do so, is not allowed to breed dogs from her country home. Some properties may have covenants that do not allow the occupier or owners to run a business from them. However, check this out with your solicitor for, very often, the rules can be bent. A type of business where people call at the house frequently is what is usually meant in such instances, not one that is run, say, with a telephone, or is a craft activity, the product of which is sold direct to shops rather than to callers at your premises.

Do you need planning permission?

Thousands of people are running businesses from their homes that are technically illegal. Why? Because they should have obtained planning permission for 'change of use' of their premises. Others should have told their mortgage company or their landlord what they were doing. Many have been doing it happily for years, and are unlikely ever to be found out, but discovery cannot be completely ruled out. And pleading ignorance of rules and regulations will not help you.

No one wants to tangle with local red tape unless it is absolutely necessary, but it would be a pity to have your thriving business closed down by vengeful officialdom because you neglected to tell them what you were doing. Bear in mind, too, that if you do need planning permission, it will take anything up to three months to come through, so start early.

Since the recession, the authorities have taken a rather more relaxed attitude to people running home businesses. So, the best thing to do is to sound out your local authorities **before you start up**, while you can still truthfully ask general rather than specific questions. In other words don't alert them by saying, 'I'm thinking of starting up a toy exchange at my house.' Instead, ring the local planning department. You'll probably get one of a number of clerks. Just ask if planning permission in general would be necessary to run such a business. They may send you a form rather than give an opinion. In that case, go to your local Citizens' Advice Bureau (see Help Section, page 178), as they may be able to help.

You do need to apply for official permission to work from home in the following situations:

- If you are proposing to add a room or a workshop, or convert your garage in some structural way. Or if you are obviously changing the use of your home, turning part of it into a tea-rooms, for instance, or a kennels.
- If you are changing the structure of the house – turning it into flats, for instance.
- If you are carrying out a business from home; actually making or repairing things, for instance, on a large and very notice-able scale.
- If you are selling things from your home on a day-to-day basis. Or if you are running, say, a beauty salon or health centre. Occasional selling parties, sporadic visits from buyers, someone having their hair done, would not count.
- If you are going to be using noisy machines or producing industrial odours that could disturb the neighbours.
- If you are going to have constant visitors in connection with your business, and cars parking at all times of the day.
- If you want to display a large permanent sign of any kind. A 'no vacancies' notice in the window would not count.
- If there are going to be any activities that are unusual for the area in which you live. Lorries arriving with supplies in the middle of a private estate would soon alert neighbours to the fact that something was going on. However, if you live in the

middle of the country or on the edge of an industrial estate, no one would be likely to notice.

You do not usually have to apply for planning permission if:

- You are running a business in your home rather than producing something. That is, if the work you do is telephone based, for instance, or you are running an agency of some kind, and therefore are not producing an end product.
- If your house is essentially still mainly your home and still looks like a residential building.
- If you do not use most of the house as a workshop or office; just one room, perhaps.
- If you do not use a lot of machines. One or two computers, a sewing machine and an overlocker would be fine. Five such machines would be looked on with suspicion.
- If business visitors to the house are sporadic. Everyone has callers, but a constant stream of people would be disruptive to others and arouse suspicion.

It's all a matter of scale. You can carry on any kind of small business without it being considered a 'change of use'. It's when you get big and successful that the problems arise. With luck, by then you will be doing so well that you're planning to take on outside premises.

Everything depends on the attitude of the neighbours. It's essential to make friends with them, and tell them what you are up to, unless you have good reason to believe they might not wish you well. Many people with home businesses adopt the ostrich technique and bury their heads in the sand of rules and regulations. They continue working that way, hoping that they don't need permission to do so, but not wanting to find out for sure. That is fine, unless a spiteful neighbour decides to 'shop' you. The people most at risk from being found out in this way are those who live in a quiet residential cul-de-sac or an 'exclusive' estate. It would be difficult to run a motor-cycle repair shop, for instance, with engines revving, without the neighbours noticing!

If the authorities do find out, they can't put you in prison. The worst that can happen is that the neighbours might complain to the council and you will be ordered to stop your activities. You could be fined, but that would only be likely if, for instance, you had built a workshop without permission, were using it for some obviously industrial activity and refused to close down when asked to do so.

If you do have to get planning permission, then the officials will tell the rating department. Someone will come and visit you, and assess how much of the house is being used for business and you will have to pay a commercial tariff for that part – a good reason for confining your activities to one room.

By-laws

There are some laws that are in the hands of the local authority and can differ from one area to another. For instance: in some parts of the country you may have to register to do work such as ear-piercing, hairdressing, or electrolysis; in others not. Usually, these by-laws are related to health and safety, not to the use of the building. Sometimes they work in your favour, laying down rules to protect you, your health and the hours you work – if you are acting as a home-worker for an outside company, for instance.

HOW TO BE A HAPPY HOME-WORKER

Learn to recognise your own work rhythms and go with them

Sue knows that she is a 'morning person', so she starts work as a writer the moment she gets up. She has probably been turning ideas over in her mind as she washes and dresses. She then stops at mid-day to cope with routine household chores and have a lunch break. 'By then, I have got several thousand words under my belt,' says Sue, 'and I can take things easier in the afternoon.'

Jim, on the other hand, is at his working best in the evenings. 'As I live on my own, I can do as I please,' he says. He spends the mornings doing routine chores (he gets the house cleaning out of the way as fast as possible), making business telephone calls and doing administration. Then he really gets down to his account-ing work in mid-afternoon, finishing in time for the 10 o'clock news on TV. Jim admits that there are occasions when he has a 'lie-in', and doesn't get up until half-past-nine, but feels that since he works late he's entitled to do so.

Give your day a proper structure

You may have to plan your time to fit in with school runs, or getting the children's tea, but structure your working day. Be professional in your approach and set yourself proper hours. Have a lunch break – don't eat sandwiches on the run – and if your work is telephone-based, switch on the answering machine during your break and don't be tempted to pick up the receiver. Shut the workroom door behind you or stow your papers away in a desk when you have finished.

Mary, who is a computer programmer, starts her day promptly at nine o'clock by phoning a friend who works at home too. 'We take it in turns to ring each other and say, "I'm just starting now ..." We don't sit and gossip, we simply motivate each other to get going. It works really well. Then on Fridays, we meet for lunch at one house or the other and discuss how the week went.'

Learn to deal firmly with interruptions

Take your work seriously and expect others to do the same. The people around you must be made to respect what you are doing, and they won't do that if *you* underrate yourself.

Your partner, if you have one, must realise that you are working at a proper job, albeit from home, even if it is not bringing in much money at this stage. He or she could perfectly well fit in with their own work odd chores like fetching the dry cleaning, and making phone calls to the builder or plumber. After all, they would have to if you weren't there. So don't become a home-worker *and* a household drudge. It will make you feel that your job is not all that important. Remember that it is!

YOUR FAMILY – HELP OR HINDRANCE?

If you've a family, they are going to be your first clients, for you are going to have to sell them the idea before you start on outside customers. They may think at first that you are out of your mind, or just indulging some whim, but when the first orders start coming in, and you take them out to celebrate, they will soon change their opinion.

It's vital to emphasise to them that this is a job that you are doing, not a hobby. It is perfectly possible to succeed even if you have a partner who is either amused or annoyed at what you are doing. Indeed, many successful businesses have been started despite, rather than with the help of, a husband or wife. James, for example, who has always been a talented painter, suddenly found himself redundant. After a depressing month writing letters and receiving turn-downs in his computer-based job, he decided to concentrate on art instead, while he still had some redundancy money to support his family.

He specialises in portraits, and started off by painting one or two local celebrities free, in exchange for being able to display the work locally as samples of what he could do. He now makes a respectable income out of his paintings, but his wife, Jane, still refers to it as 'your mess', and resents the time he spends in his make-shift studio.

Getting them on your side

Involve the family from the word go. They're never too young to start. My granddaughter Jessica has been helping to lay the breakfast table at our holiday centre since she was four. Now she does it on her own. Toddlers can be kept occupied and happy, 'helping' a home cook with a piece of spare pastry and a board.

The most important person in any company, in my opinion, is not the managing director but the one up front – whoever sits at the reception desk or answers the phone. And as your business grows, you are going to have to gently train those around you in phone behaviour. I remember trying to contact a talented painter from whom I wanted to buy a picture. Unfortunately, the enterprise foundered because every time I rang her up I got a recalcitrant teenage son who quite obviously could not be bothered to take a message. I gave up in the end and she lost a sale.

Fortunately, there is a simple cure: buy an answering machine and keep it plugged in whenever you, personally, are not at home. If family members rush to the phone before you (a teenage habit) train them to answer in a bright, welcoming voice. Bribe them, if necessary, giving them a small percentage if you close the deal!

Coping with the children

The children must respect what you are doing too. You may build your day around them, but they have to learn that if they answer the phone, they do so in a responsible manner. And that your work-place is sacrosanct – they are not allowed to touch tools, papers, machines. Background noises of shrieks, dogs barking, sounds of riotous play are a hazard to any home worker who is trying to convince customers that he or she is a professional. So, a cordless phone is a really worthwhile investment if you have a noisy young family. You can then walk away into a quiet corner of the house, or even go and sit in the car to handle business calls.

If you have small children to cope with and have friends and neighbours in a similar position, organise a rota system so that you take in each other's kids. Or this could be a job opportunity for someone! Have a supply of videos handy for emergency situations. Most children will sit through two before complaining that they are bored.

Coralling pets

This is especially important if you have people calling at the house. You may love king pussums with his funny little ways, but your visitors may not. I remember a hilarious moment when a solemn young man from the local Council called to interview me for a survey. As he sat alongside me on the settee, both the cat and the dog climbed on his lap and refused to get off. I'm glad I was not trying to sell him something!

Making it work

Working from home is not like working in an office. You don't have the discipline of set hours. You will have to train yourself not to be untidy and turn the entire house into an office or workshop with things strewn all over the place. And if you have been used to being told what to do you may find it difficult at first to motivate yourself and get started. There's a temptation to make too many cups of tea in the morning before you get going. At home, there are so many distractions: beds unmade, the lawn to be cut, the washing up to be done. You can easily crowd out your working hours with chores.

You will also have to cultivate staying power, especially in those later weeks when the first enthusiasm has worn off. And you have to think constantly in terms of priorities – which jobs need doing first. No one else is going to tell you. In many ways, it is easier to go to a place of work; having people labouring alongside you makes it easier to get started and to persist. And if you've chosen a solitary kind of job you may, at first, find you're suffering from a lack of company. But that should soon pass. After all, you're simply changing gear.

These hurdles all need to be overcome, and you'll do it that much more easily if you've chosen the right job for your personality.

If you are going to run a business where people need to visit your home, one basic thing that you ought to have is a down-stairs lavatory. It's embarrassing to have to show people through the house to an upstairs bathroom, especially if the beds are unmade and the bedroom doors wide open! But, if they have come some way to see you, a request to use the lavatory at some stage is almost inevitable.

If you don't have a downstairs cloakroom, remember that now it is possible to plumb in a lavatory easily in all sorts of situations. You can buy models which have an electric pump system attached, which means that they don't have to be installed right next to the water and sewage system.

MOTIVATING YOURSELF

If you find it hard to start work each day – and it happens to all of us – then try these tricks to get going.

As you have breakfast, do a little harmless day-dreaming about how successful you are going to be, think of the car you're going to buy when you get your first break, how envious your friends are going to be.

Leave a project unfinished at the end of the day ... a novel in mid-sentence, a letter half written, a toy partly made. You will know exactly what you have to get on with when you start work the next morning and that ushers you into the day.

Paying yourself

If you're employed by someone else, you can stop at intervals to chat with your colleagues, discuss last night's TV or the football final over a cup of coffee. All this time you are still getting paid. You can fall ill for a day or so, and know that your wages are still coming in. Or you can spend a day walled up in time-consuming meetings, without having actually produced anything, secure in your salary. You can also use the office stationery in as extravagant a way as you please, and the telephone, making long business calls at peak times without worrying about the bill. Similarly, if there's a problem with the computer or the photostat machine, even your car if it is a company one, you know someone else will foot the repair bill. But from now on, as a home-worker, you're going to have to keep an eye on the economy side of things. You're working life is going to be leaner – and all the more healthy.

Using your time

You're going to have to be strict, in future, with casual visitors who will otherwise eat into your working time. Let friends and neighbours know what you are doing from the start, so they will respect your business hours and not gossip over the phone or over a cup of coffee. Don't forget to be equally strict with yourself, but plan for a proper time off. Weekends and evenings should not see you slaving away, unless you are just starting up or fulfilling a rush order. If your business activities leave you no time to relax, they need re-thinking.

Making a start

You have made the decision to work from home. You know what you want to do, you have researched it properly and you are sure there is a market for it. Now comes the time to start, and the first thing to do is to set up your place of work.

A room that you can shut behind you when the day's work is done is the best possible workplace to have. Failing that, a discreet desk in a corner of the living room may well be all you need. Think creatively about which room will become your work centre. Let a room in your house lead a secret double life: Lisa, a hairdresser needed a washbasin for shampooing her clients' hair, as her bathroom was too narrow for the purpose. So she installed one in the corner of her bedroom and made that room her salon. Her dressing table makes a perfect centre for blow-drying and styling, and when the room is not in salon use (equipment is stored at the bottom of the wardrobe), the washbasin is still a useful asset.

Mary, a dressmaker, uses her large farmhouse-style kitchen as her workroom, but you would never know it. The long pull-out table is perfect for cutting out on, and the sewing machine stows away in a bottom kitchen cupboard when evening comes. Half-finished garments are hung in plastic bags in a closet in the hall. In the hall, too, is a simple painted chest in which she stows fabric, silks and cottons, needles and pins.

Another great potential source of space is the garage, if you have somewhere else to stow garden tools and all the other impedimenta that is usually found inside. Vicky runs a thriving business from home, dealing in children's second-hand clothes. And every weekend her garage becomes a temporary shop. She has bought some garment rails on wheels, the kind that are offered for sale in the small-ads in the papers and publications like *Exchange and Mart*. These are easily dismantled and stowed away, so during the week she keeps them stacked in the cupboard under the stairs. Come the weekend, the rails are put together and wheeled out to the garage to display the clothes.

There are all sorts of other spaces that you could use as a work area, apart from the traditional spare bedroom. A disused garden shed could easily be converted into a workroom. The roof might need insulating from extremes of heat or cold but any handyman or woman could do that easily, nailing up sheets of glass fibre wool. You could run electricity out to it simply by buying a plug-in spool of waterproof cable, available from any DIY warehouse. For any work of a more complicated nature, do consult a professional electrician. The attic, too, with the help of a loft ladder makes another potential working space, especially if you put in a skylight.

THE CLOTHES YOU WEAR

The whole concept of your wardrobe changes if you decide to work from home. Unless you are actually having clients to the house, working as a solicitor, accountant or in any other professional capacity, you can relax!

Don't fall into the trap, however, of wearing out old clothes: scruffy trousers that were due at the cleaner's a long time ago, or stained sweaters. If you do, you'll find it has a psychological effect on you and your work after a time.

If you're wearing casual clothes, they should be attractive ones. Mary, who works all day at her computer, says, 'Since I'm sitting down most of the time, I don't want anything with tight waistbands or unyielding fabric. I find loose, warm clothing such as tracksuits are ideal. I have three, in bright colours that make me feel good when I wear them. At any given time I have one in the wash, one drying and one on. And when evening comes and the family are around, I change into something else.'

Designated work clothes make you feel more professional – a sleeveless jerkin if you're gardening, a bright smock if you're working on a craft, an overall with pockets for pins if you're dressmaking, all make you feel as if you are 'going to work' when you put them on.

Making Your House Work For You

Is letting your game? ... Where do you live? ... What have you got to offer? ... What kind of customers can you expect? ... Taking in tourists ... Living with your lodgers ... Letting the whole house

TAKING IN LODGERS, letting off bed-sitters or even dividing the building into flats are all ways in which you can make your house work for you if you have rooms to spare. Using your home as a source of income has the great advantage that it is a passive occupation, rather than a full-time job. If you have lodgers or bed-sitter tenants, provided you are organised, you can carry on living your own life alongside your house guests. If you *are* able to convert part of the building into a self-contained flat, that is even better, for the tenants should hardly impinge on your life at all.

Before embarking on any of these enterprises as a business rather than on a casual scale, however, check that you are not infringing the terms of your mortgage or, if you are renting the property, that the landlord will not object. And if you convert part of the house you will almost certainly need planning permission, which is seldom withheld these days (see Help Section, page 190).

If you are rattling around in a very large house and have the right contacts, it might pay you to consider applying for permission to turn it into, say, a language school or a centre for alternative medicine. Cynthia, a widow who has a rambling house in south east London, thought of the alternative medicine centre idea when her osteopath told her that the lease on the rooms where he practised was up and he was looking for somewhere to go. Cynthia offered him two rooms in her house, and very soon afterwards let off more space to contacts of his in the fringe medicine field. She had to get planning permission, of course, and has converted the top floor of the house into a flat for herself. 'It has changed my life,' she says. 'Now, at last, I have a reasonable income and security.'

IS LETTING YOUR GAME?

How are you going to like having strangers in your house? If you've never taken in paying guests or let rooms before, it's a good idea to start by taking people on a strictly short-term basis to see how you get on.

If you have a family or a partner around, it's obvious that you will need their backing before you contemplate taking in other people. Resentful, surly teenagers could soon scupper any plans to take in tourists, for instance.

Or you may have to work around them. If you've a tiny baby or toddler for instance, you are probably better simply letting off rooms rather than attempting to provide any services. Although you might be lucky, like Anne and Jeremy, who found that they had got themselves some willing resident baby-sitters!

Even if you live alone, the scheme may not go entirely well. Margery, a retired civil servant, lived by herself and decided to take in lodgers partly for cash, partly for company. But when they actually moved in, her reaction was not at all what she had expected.

'I was surprised to find how much I resented the invasion of my privacy,' she says. 'Every time I walked out of the living room I seemed to pass someone in the hall. I felt trapped, claustrophobic. I hadn't realised before, I was in the habit of walking round the house in my dressing-gown or with un-combed hair. Now I felt I had to dress up for them. And I hated all their bits in my bathroom – razors, shampoos and all that. I tried telling myself, "You're earning good money doing this," but it didn't help.' She decided to give up letting, and do part-time work instead to supplement her pension.

WHERE DO YOU LIVE?

Whom you get as lodgers or tenants and how much you can charge them will depend very much on your surroundings. So the first thing you need to do is to assess the actual situation of your home, for it's no good planning to take in paying guests if they don't want or need to come to your area in the first place. But, if that's your situation, all is not lost – there may well be other ways of attracting custom.

Are you in or near a large city?

The larger the city, the more pressure there is on accommo-dation, and if you live in or near one, you should have no difficulty in letting rooms all year round. There are so many groups of people you can tap into from among business, pro-fessional and academic sources. In fact, you should be in the happy position of being able to pick and choose the type of lodger you house.

Is yours a University town?

If so, you have a regular supply of students on tap, many of whom are desperate for somewhere to stay, for few colleges and universities have anywhere near enough accommodation of their own. And, in any case, most students prefer the freedom of living out of halls after the first year.

The peak time for finding college student lodgers is usually in late summer. This is when they know whether or not they have been accepted, and start looking for digs. The best way to find students is to contact the colleges and put cards up on their notice boards. Most academic complexes have a Student's Union, and this is a good organisation to get in touch with for possible lodgers. It is very likely that the college will send along someone to vet your premises before adding you to their contacts list. This would be an opportunity for you to raise any queries *you* may have. Ask around and look at cards in windows offering rooms to rent to get an idea of what you should charge.

Taking in anyone connected with the academic year means that there are times like mid-summer when your rooms would not be occupied. Some people charge a token rent if the student wants to retain the room, others don't bother. However, if yours is a well known university town, it should be possible to fill in with another type of guest – people coming to the centre, often from abroad, for summer schools and conferences. These are becoming more and more popular and as the numbers increase it is not always possible to put up everyone in hall, so outside accommodation is often needed.

Is there an industrial estate on your doorstep?

If so, you would have no difficulty in letting accommodation, either, since there should be a large work-force to draw on. With so many companies re-locating to new areas, people are often shunted from one end of the country to another and need somewhere to stay while they hunt for a new home. Usually it is the employee only, but sometimes there might be families looking for accommodation while their new house is being made ready for them.

There could also be a thriving business to be had from taking in trainees who are brought into your area for a short time. Many firms these days run courses for their staff at head office. And if head office happens to be near you, get in touch; they may well be glad to know you have rooms to spare. The person to contact in the first instance would be the personnel officer. These training courses can last anything from a long weekend to a month. And short-term lets like these often attract higher rents than those on a more permanent basis, since they are paid for by the employers.

What about the DSS?

With so many unemployed and homeless people around it's a sad fact of life that many of them end up in bed and breakfast accommodation paid for by the DSS (formerly the DHSS). If you are planning to set up a proper bed and breakfast business and would be prepared to take in families in this situation, contact your local Housing Department for further details.

Is your area attractive to tourists?

Foreign visitors to Britain are becoming more adventurous than they used to be, and have started fanning out from the obvious places like London, Edinburgh, Stratford-upon-Avon to visit other attractive areas – one of them could be yours.

The best way to get on the tourist trail, is to make yourself known to the local Tourist Board (see page 190), who will no doubt be glad to hear of you and put you on their books. Bear in mind, however, that if you want to put up a sign outside your house offering something: bed and breakfast for instance, you will need to check out the local authority rules (see page 190). Advertising yourself in this way means that you are likely to have travellers arriving on your doorstep at all times of day, so be prepared. There needs to be someone at home all day in case they should call on you unexpectedly, needing a room.

WHAT HAVE YOU GOT TO OFFER?

First assess the accommodation you're working with. How many rooms do you have to spare? Do you want to let them all?

If so, what are you going to do if friends want to stay? Do any of the rooms have washbasins of their own? If not, and you are thinking of letting on a permanent basis, is it possible to have some installed? Sometimes the hot water supply is a problem, but you can now buy small over-the-sink electric heaters which provide hot water instantly as you need it, and are easy to fix.

Bathrooms

Think, too, about the bathroom scene. With only one bathroom in the house, which has to be shared with the family, you could not take on more than two tenants with any comfort, even if they were out all day. And how tidy are the family going to be about leaving the bathroom fit for a paying guest to use? Maybe they will need some training on that front.

If, on the other hand, you are on your own, you might be able to take in more than two lodgers with a shared bathroom. However, if you are taking on letting or paying guests as a business, and you're staying put in a house with plenty of rooms to spare, might it not be worthwhile to turn one into an extra bathroom? This sort of conversion work is definitely worth while as it improves the value of a property if you should decide eventually to sell.

Bed-sitters

Letting off bed-sitting rooms rather than taking in lodgers has one great advantage: your tenants are more independent of you. They don't have to share your living space in the evenings and be one of the family. So, if the spare rooms in your house are spacious enough, it may pay to turn them into bed-sitters, although initially they will cost you more to set up.

Each room needs to be large enough to accommodate a bed (which could be one that converts into a sofa), an armchair, a table and two chairs. Unless you are willing and able to share your kitchen, it will need some sort of cooking facility and a small fridge. Even if they are cooking alongside you anyway, a small fridge in their room is a good idea since it segregates their food from yours.

It is perfectly possible for several bed-sitter tenants to share the main kitchen if you are a relaxed cook. But it is far better if they share separate cooking facilities with each other, or, best of all, if they can all cook in their own rooms. The simplest facilities for this are a plug-in electric kettle and a microwave – some models offer the choice of conventional cooking, too. Be sure to cover the wall where the cooker is, either with tiles or with a sponge-down surface, and if the room is carpeted invest in a clear plastic runner (on sale in carpeting shops) to cover it at the working area. The room should also have a small TV set and a radio, and reasonable lighting. Several low-placed lamps are better, any time, than a single depressing 25 watt bulb hanging overhead – the sort of lighting that I had to put up with when I lived in a bed-sitter.

Even if you are using cheap or second-hand furniture, do your best to make the bed-sitters look as attractive as possible. It costs very little to put in bright new cushions, lampshades and tablecloths, for instance, and to include things like a waste-paper basket, and a bedside lamp. Mary, who decided to convert her house into bed-sits, made a point of sleeping overnight in each room before she let it. That's the easiest and best way to find out whether it is comfortable or not! Your tenants will respond by keeping the room in much better condition than if it was squalid and run-down.

Conversions

If you are planning to let off several bed-sits, consider the possibility of converting an area of the corridor outside into a mini-kitchen. Rambling Edwardian and Victorian houses quite often have unusually wide landings and hallways, or corners where it might be possible to conjure something up. It is possible to buy a complete mini-kitchen: a small stainless-steel sink, and a drainer with two electric rings and a refrigerator beneath it, all housed in what looks like a sink unit. For an extra sum there is even a tiny dishwasher which goes under the sink. A set-up like this, with a microwave/conventional oven mounted on the wall above will give you all the facilities you need to offer, and you could easily fit it into a space about 3ft 6in wide (just over a metre). However, if you are installing electric cooking rings or a conventional oven, you'll need to fix an extractor fan overhead or the whole area will become covered in grease very quickly and cooking smells will permeate the whole house.

If you're thinking of doing any kind of conversion work, remember that you may need planning permission (see Help Section, page 190), so check it out before you start. If you need to get the experts in, rather than tackling it on a DIY basis, get more than one estimate for the job. You may be surprised to find there is a wide divergence in prices, and you may save yourself some cash. Also, ask if you may see photographs of previous work done by the architect or builder. Professionals are usually used to this sort of request and happy to meet it; if they are not, think again.

Bear in mind, also, that a house that is split into a number of flats decreases in value from the point of view of the housing market, unless you are planning to sell off the flats separately.

Lodgers

If you're simply taking in lodgers, and the rooms are already furnished adequately with a bed, chair, somewhere to write, and somewhere to stow their clothes, extra bed linen is all you will need. Save time and trouble by buying sheets, duvet covers and pillowcases made from a 50/50 per cent polyester/cotton mix. It is by far the best choice since it dries quickly and needs no ironing. And it's essential if you are going to have a quick turn-over, doing bed and breakfast, for instance.

Getting equipped

Don't skimp on details like pillows and mattresses. It's better to buy new ones if yours are stained. You know that stain is only a spilled cup of tea, but your tenants might be put off!

Go for cheap and cheerful linen and towels, and replace them frequently. The best places to look for these are chains such as the Swedish firm IKEA, and the Argos catalogue shops. They are also good for small things like lamps and bedside tables.

If you are turning the house into bed-sitters or flats you may need to buy things like cookers and fridges. Here, it is definitely worth while hunting around for second-hand equipment which sells at a fraction of the price of new items. Glassware, cutlery and crockery, however, is better bought new in packs at amazingly cheap prices from places like Argos, and you will not be too upset if things get broken. Choose patterns that you know are going to be repeated, so you can replace them easily.

If you are short of space, look for stack-away furniture. There's a special table which is permanently advertised in mail order catalogues and seen around in many shops too. It has two large drop leaves which, when they are both down turn it into a narrow side table about 1ft wide. With it come four foldable chairs which stow away under the top – ideal for a small flat or bed-sitter.

To make your accommodation seem more home-like you will need a few ornaments and rugs. The place to go for these is events like car boot sales or to second-hand, rather than antique, shops. If you've an eye for sorting through junk, you'll be surprised how quickly you can assemble a room that looks co-ordinated and attractive.

WHAT KIND OF CUSTOMERS CAN YOU EXPECT

Having carefully assessed your own situation, and the type of accommodation you can offer, what can you expect of your prospective clients?

The flat and bed-sitter brigade

Provided you have a proper lease drawn up, renting out part of the house as a flat is the most trouble free way of having people under your roof. Failing that, properly equipped bed-sitting rooms should bring you equally trouble-free tenants. You need, of course, to have a large house to do this. And you may have to spend out capital in the first place to equip the accommodation (see above). But over the months you should quickly recoup your outlay.

Lodgers, or paying guests

Many different categories of people want to rent rooms as lodgers, sharing your kitchen to prepare their own meals. There are businessmen and women who find themselves working away from home, for instance. In this case they will tend to go off early in the morning, come home early evening and perhaps go out again, and be away at weekends. This category of paying guest is probably the most trouble-free, and should have no difficulty meeting the rent. But if you want someone to chat to from time to time, you may well be out of luck.

Single 9 to 5 workers come next in the trouble-free stakes. They tend to be around at weekends but are likely to have organised themselves a fairly heavy social life and will, therefore, not be under your feet all the time. Both these categories can be taken in without impinging much on your daily life. Both are likely to need somewhere safe to park a car.

The third category are people without regular hours. Students, for instance, who may be at home studying for part of the day, and professionals – people who work all kinds of shifts round the clock – actors, journalists, social workers, probation officers, doctors and nurses in particular. Their presence in your house would be more noticeable than in the case of the 9 to 5 set. Renee, an ex-nurse, specialises in taking in people from the local hospital, for instance.

'I like to have students or young doctors staying with me,' she says. 'It keeps me in touch with the medical world and we can talk the same shop. I also understand the long, erratic hours they have to work, something that some landladies would find difficult to come to terms with.'

Many of Renee's lodgers are on night duty some of the time. She has them on a paying guest basis, but also provides meals for most of them – often at unusual hours – supper as late as 10 or 11 o'clock at night, for instance.

'If they're really going to be late, I leave some soup to be heated up and sandwiches,' says Renee, who has never married and feels that her students are her 'family'. 'I agonise with them over exam results, and if somebody fails, I feel as bad about it as if it's happening to me!'

Bed and breakfast

Bed and breakfast, whether it is on a regular or just a short-term basis will bring in more cash than lodgers or straightforward letting, provided you have a good supply of people to draw on. And since you are probably getting breakfast for the family every day, it adds very little extra work.

To make bed and breakfast really successful, it's best to have a separate bathroom for your visitors, or at least a washbasin in their room, so they don't collide with the rest of a household in the morning rush. And you'll need a good supply of bed linen and sheets – as I've already said, the non-iron, quick drying polyester/cotton mix is best. Bed and breakfast means just that, and you are not obliged to provide a separate sitting room with TV. But if you are going for long-term stays, then you will need, probably, to put a small television set in the bedroom.

TAKING IN TOURISTS

If you are interested in taking in visitors from abroad and your area is right for them, most Tourist authorities (see Help Section, page 190) run a free registration scheme that you could join, with a grading system for accommodation. You will be asked to tell them what facilities you have, and what you are prepared to offer in the way of services. They will then probably send an inspector to check out your accommodation before you are put on their books.

Once you are part of this scheme you can ask to be officially graded. And then you will be included in the many promotions that they run, and perhaps listed in their leaflets.

You could also let it be known at the town hall, at local places which tourists are likely to visit: petrol service stations, local pubs and restaurants, for instance. Contact them and tell them that you have rooms to let or that you do bed and breakfast. They will be glad to hear about you so that they can send you the overflow. If you're an enthusiastic cook, consider doing an evening meal for your guests, featuring local specialities or homing in on traditional recipes – your Tourist Board will help you again, in this direction.

Extra services

Tell your visitors when they arrive what services you're willing to provide. You may offer to give them early morning tea, for instance, though an easy way round that is to supply them with an electric kettle, teapot, and sachets of tea, coffee, sugar and powdered milk. If you are willing to do extra things like laundering their clothes for them, mention this. Many visitors are touring by car and have difficulty over laundry. Offer something extra in the way of service. Collect leaflets on places to visit, local tours, and have them ready for your visitors. You could also steer them in the direction of the right gift shops to visit – and possibly get a small commission from the shop concerned if they buy. Maybe you or your friends make craft items or paint landscapes of the area. If so, display them tactfully in the house; you might well make a few sales.

People from 'new' countries like the USA and the antipodes are fascinated by our history, which is so much longer than theirs. And if you can communicate your enthusiasm for your locality to them, you will have made their holiday that much happier. They will also almost certainly pass your address on to their friends.

Historic houses

If you are lucky enough to own a house that is of historic interest, than you have a potential gold-mine. In this case, it is well worth while decorating your guest rooms in period style with tourists in mind. Compile a history of the house and have it on hand for them to read; it might even be worth having a small leaflet printed to be distributed to local gift shops, information centres and pubs.

Denis, who lives in a restored Georgian house in London, has found a novel way of making it earn its keep. He has restored it to exactly the way it was in the 18th century, to the extent of hiding any evidence of modern inventions like electricity (though a tape recorder hidden under the floorboards which plays sounds like the clip-clopping of horses, and the calls of street vendors belies the fact). His house is not full of priceless antiques, but much of the 'furniture' has been specially made in Georgian style for him, to fit in with the surroundings.

Denis doesn't have people to stay but he offers an evening tour of his candle-lit house. He gives his visitors a history lesson on the spot, telling them what the life of a mythical family was like in those times. He is a favourite stop on the American tourist circuit, and has attracted a lot of publicity on TV and in newspapers and magazines.

If your house has a pedigree, be it Elizabethan, Jacobean or Georgian, and you're prepared to put up with the inconvenience of living in what is basically a museum, there could be good money to be made using it in the way that Denis has. Being shown round a real house, rather than a stately home where everything is behind glass or roped off, could be a really attractive experience for foreign visitors. Your local Tourist Board would be able to advise you on how long your tour should be, and what you should charge. If you could offer a 'period' meal as well, it could be quite a lucrative business.

Casual visitors

Taking in casual visitors means that you may have to produce meals unexpectedly, so it makes sense to cook and freeze dishes in advance, then heat them up at the last minute in a microwave, so these are two items of equipment you'll need. With a fast turn-over of people, you may also need to augment your stocks of bed-linen and towels.

Fix your prices according to the going rate – check it out with the Tourist Board. You will have to decide from the outset whether you are going to charge by the person or by the room, French style, and whether you'll charge extra if a single person occupies a double room.

If you have four bedrooms or more to let, or are taking in at least eight people, you are required by law to display a notice giving the maximum and minimum prices per night. The usual place to put this is on the back of the bedroom door. Hotels usually demand payment in advance from casual visitors. You should at least charge a deposit.

Student tourists

Another source of income on the tourist front could be taking in foreign students who are studying at a local college or language school. For more on this subject see Section Seven, page 164.

LIVING WITH YOUR LODGERS

If you've been used to living alone, or as a quiet, well regulated couple, taking in others to share your home can be a stressful business. If, on the other hand you are an easy-going family well used to having friends drop in, then you will almost certainly be able to assimilate extra people without a qualm. Either way, you may well find that you need to be more flexible in your thinking, taking strangers on board. 'Start as you mean to go on' used to be the standard advice to newly-weds, and the same applies to the business of taking lodgers into your house.

Of course, having someone else in your house can be a

rewarding experience rather than a trial: I had a wonderful young lodger called Henry who stayed with me for eight years, and even moved house with me. He has now become a life-long friend. Others are not so lucky: a cousin of mine, Penny, who was on the verge of bankruptcy, took in a young spoiled Parisienne as a paying guest because she badly needed the money. She found herself summoned, each morning, to help decide which couture dress Marie-France should wear. Penny, meanwhile, couldn't afford the price of a pair of tights ...

Smoking

One fundamental point you will have to decide, early on, is whether or not you are prepared to take smokers in the house. If cigarettes appear on your weekly shopping list this will be no problem, but if you don't smoke you may well find you do not like sharing with people who do. This happened to Bill:

'I gave up smoking ten years ago. It was a struggle, but I managed it eventually. Then, this winter I took in a friend whose wife had left him. I'd forgotten that he smoked – you didn't notice if you just saw it in the pub, or at football. Anyway, I found I just couldn't stand having him in the house because of his cigarettes. Far from wanting to smoke again, the fumes made me choke. Eventually I had to give him an ultimatum – either smoke outside, or go.' (See also under: *The Student Scene*, as any or all of these situations/considerations are relevant for other types of guest or boarder.)

The student scene

Taking in students can be an experience that is both exhilarating and exhausting. In having them in your house, you become part parent, part counsellor, and sometimes part disciplinarian. Be prepared to offer a shoulder to cry on when their love life or their study scene goes wrong. You may also have to be tactful enough not to ask what is the matter if they show no inclination to tell you.

Friends

If you have a clutch of students in your house, it's essential to make some good-humoured but firm rules and stick to them. You must decide, for instance, whether or not boy/girlfriends are allowed in their rooms. Legally, you cannot stop them having visitors, but these do not have to turn into overnight stays, and there could come a time when you wonder whether you are letting a room for one or for two. No doubt they will have their own front door keys, but you may find it necessary to impose some sort of reasonable curfew. If yours is a small house, the sound of a drunken merrymaker crashing in at three in the morning may pall, after a time. However students are not the only culprits: Joan agreed to put up a visiting rugby team who were playing several matches in the area – and lived to rue the day!

One man's music ...

You may also feel you have to make some sort of ruling on loud music. It's not just the actual sound. Alan, who lets out a basement flat in his Manchester house to a pop music fiend, finds it's not the music itself that bothers him but the thump thump thump of the beat which comes through the walls and gives him a headache. These days, in the era of personal stereos, Walkmans and headphones, there is no excuse for playing blaring music that other people can hear after hours.

Telephone trouble

One of the biggest headaches over taking in lodgers is the question of the telephone. You may ask them to note down their calls but, with the best will in the world you can be sure that some will slip by.

In short, phoning is one of the biggest potential areas for dispute, when you have people in your home. They may say they have had three minutes calling Newcastle, worse still New York. But you'll feel resentful if you suspect they are not being accurate, and you can't very well call them liars. But no doubt an escalating phone bill may well confirm you are right.

British Telecom can come to the rescue here. You can, of course, put a block on out-going calls by various means. If you are taking in paying guests in a serious way, it pays to invest in a BT pay-phone. The latest models are very compact; one would soon pay for itself in savings on your phone bill. Don't forget to keep a bag of cash handy so that you can give your charges some change as they need it. If you are letting off flats, then it is common sense to make sure the tenants have their own phones. If you are letting flats on a short-term basis, then you could own the lines, but get the calls monitored and charged for the period of occupancy. Contact British Telecom for help in this direction.

Rent

You will have to decide whether you are going to charge the rent weekly or monthly (it's best to fit in with times when the tenant's wages are paid). You should be business-like and buy a rent book. The rent should be paid in advance, to avoid your tenant getting away with a 'moonlight flit'. If you are letting furnished accommodation, that is, a bedsitter or a flat, rather than taking in a lodger, then you should also charge a returnable deposit to cover breakages. It's wise to take out extra insurance for what the French call 'responsabilité civile' to make sure you are covered should your tenant fall down your stairs and break a leg, or have some possession ruined by fire, water, or some other accident. Tell your insurance broker or company that you are taking in tenants and let them advise you.

References

By all means ask for references, but don't set too much store by them, unless they come from a source such as the tenant's bank, for these are easily forged. It is better to make up your own mind whether the person who wants the room is someone that you feel you could share your house with. We all make mistakes, but since you live in the house yourself as owner/occupier, any problem over getting rid of a tenant should not arise, for they can be given 'reasonable notice' to quit if things go wrong.

LETTING THE WHOLE HOUSE

One very bold decision you could take, particularly if you are retired would be to let your home in its entirety and stay somewhere cheaper. Robert and Mary do just that for six moths of the year, and end up in profit.

'I've always suffered from rheumatism,' says Mary. 'And I've found that living somewhere like the South of Spain is definitely better for me in winter.' They homed in on the area around Almeira, which is said to have the driest climate in Europe, and soon found they could rent a flat there at a knock-down price during the winter time.

Now Robert and Mary let their London flat from October to March and spend the winter in Spain. 'We make a good profit on the deal,' says Robert. "We rent through an agency who deal mainly in people who are coming to Britain from the Middle East, and sometimes from American or Australia. They come to London for all kinds of things – for the theatre, for medical treatment, or to see relatives. The agency takes 15 per cent of the rent, and for that money they clean the flat, change the bed-linen and so on. We don't have to do a thing, though naturally we lock away all our best ornaments, and china.'

Cooking from Home

The rules before you start ... First check out your equipment ... Buying your produce ... What are you going to cook? ... Selling yourself and your products ... Catering for others ... Lunch and dinner parties ... Finger food ... The sandwich scene ... Home baking ... Selling from stalls ... Cooking for restaurants, wine bars and pubs ... Preserves, pickles and chutneys ... Sweets and confectionery ... Special occasion food ... Weddings and christenings ... Fun cakes ... Childrens' party packages ... Club events ... Foreign food ... Food for photography and filming ... Writing cookbooks ... Hiring out equipment ... The social cook ... Costing ... right ... Insurance ... Transport

THIS SECTION is specially for you if you really love food, and feel frustrated that you don't have enough scope for your talent for cooking. If you're a really dedicated cook, then you would get great creative satisfaction out of selling your services in some way, *and* make some useful cash. A career in cookery can easily be run from home if you have a flair with food. You don't need any formal training to get started – though a library of cookbooks will help. And you will already have most of the basic equipment to hand. It is also something you can start up alone, bringing in extra helpers as and when you need them – for special events, for instance.

You may decide that you want to prepare something in batches and sell it on to another caterer, from a market stall or through shops. Or you may want to give a more personal service and cook for other people's parties, or club events. It depends on your particular talents and your personality. And it *is* possible to cook for a living today, despite scare stories you may have heard about the new hygiene legislation. So let's get the official business out of the way.

THE RULES BEFORE YOU START

The official hygiene regulations regarding food are simple enough for anyone to understand and comply with. They really amount to no more than simple caution and common sense. If you run a food business you have a particular responsibility to keep the product you make and sell clean and safe. And you are dealing basically with the *Food Safety Act* of 1990, which says it is an offence for anyone to 'sell or process for sale food which is harmful to health, contaminated to such an extent that it would be unreasonable to expect it to be eaten, falsely described, or not what the customer can reasonably expect'.

Your kitchen

Your premises must be suitable, easily cleaned, well ventilated, properly lit, and have 'adequate facilities for hygiene'. This means your kitchen should have wipe-clean work surfaces such as stainless steel, ceramic tiles, or a laminated surface. Environmental health officers do not like wood, for the obvious reason that microbes can lurk in its fibres, so you'll have to stow away your decorative chopping boards and get something plain and laminated (see the Help Section, page 191, for publications that will help you).

There must be 'adequate space for rubbish to be temporarily

stored', and no refuse should be allowed to accumulate in the kitchen except 'so far as may be unavoidable for the proper carrying on of the trade or business.' There should not be a lavatory leading directly off the kitchen, and there must be a convenient hand washbasin (not in the kitchen) with hot and cold running water, and soap. You must keep as clean as possible in all parts of yourself and your clothing that are liable to come into contact with food. You must keep any open cuts or abrasions on any exposed part of yourself covered with a suitable waterproof dressing. And you must refrain from smoking.

All these regulations make sense to anyone who is a serious cook, and they are not likely to cause you problems. It goes without saying that it is vital, of course, to have an adequately sized kitchen and the right equipment, if you're cooking in bulk, unless you want to feel like a galley slave. To keep the inspector happy, your kitchen should have proper ventilation – probably an extractor fan over the cooker. It must also have a double sink.

Environmental health

The only other thing you have to do before starting up is to register with the Local Environmental Health Department at least a month before you start up the business. Registration is free. (See Help Section, page 191 for details on where you can get more information on this subject). It pays to make an appointment to go and see the local Environmental Health officer (don't just turn up unannounced), and tell him or her what you are planning to do. In general these people are very helpful. If you are replanning the kitchen or starting it from scratch, think about the projected work flow, and make sure everything is sited so that you can move from one piece of equipment to the next without unnecessary zig-zagging around the room. It may be hard on the feet, but not particularly trying to have an ill-planned kitchen when you are working by yourself. But it takes the addition of just one helper for a frantic cooking session to result in constant collisions.

The food

Very basically, the rules say that you must keep raw and cooked food apart. This might mean buying a second fridge. You must use clean packing materials – the easiest way round this is to use disposable plastic and foil containers, and cling-wrap and aluminium foil rather than returnable dishes. Before these laws came into effect, I remember seeing a galvanised bucket of cooked beef and veg – destined as a filling for pies – left on the doorstep of a popular restaurant in Covent Garden before opening time. I don't think they'd get away with that now!

As far as the food itself goes, remember that germs are not active at very high or very low temperatures, so for safety's sake you're going to need to cool your produce as fast as you can after cooking to avoid possible contamination. To keep your mind at rest, you should also buy a thermometer for the 'fridge to make sure that food is kept at the prescribed temperature below 5 degrees.

Food also should not be stored in a room that contains animal feed (pets are, of course, banned). And it should not be stored at a height of less than 18in (45.5 cm) from the ground unless it is 'adequately protected'.

Remember you're going to need somewhere to store basic dry goods like sugar and flour which you'll be buying in bulk. And you must be vigilant about 'use by' dates of things that have a shorter life. It goes without saying that anything you freeze and pack must be meticulously labelled and dated. There is nothing more infuriating than fumbling among a heap of identical grey parcels wondering which one is raspberry purée and which is soup!

Using the garden

If you've a garden, plan now to grow your own herbs and garnishes – for example, chives, parsley and mint, which you can cut as you need. Not only will you save time and money going to the shops at the last minute for, say a bunch of chives, but, if they are freshly picked, they will wilt less quickly when they're on display as a garnish.

FIRST CHECK OUT YOUR EQUIPMENT

When I first started running Arts in Provence, and took in people for courses, I found myself cooking for at least twelve every day instead of just one or two. I'd had the common sense to make sure I had the crockery, cutlery and napkins I needed, but the first week was frantic, as I scrabbled around the cupboards looking for large-sized saucepans and serving dishes. Don't attempt to start cooking on a large scale without making sure you have what you need. There's nothing more alarming than having a huge pan of pasta on the boil and nothing to decant it into.

As you are now going to have to present food to the public, get into the habit of looking out for unusual serving dishes at car boot sales, in junk shops, at auctions. (But remember that anything with a crack in it would be frowned upon by the local Environmental Health authorities). You will soon build up a collection of things for next to nothing; few people these days want to possess large-sized dishes and are happy to get rid of them. It's worth while looking for crockery and cutlery too, there are some amazing bargains to be had at auction sales.

You may belong to the school of cooks who boast all they need is a sharp knife and a wooden spoon, but if you are going into catering, you will need extra oven racks, baking tins, saucepans, serving dishes and things like colanders. When equipping yourself from scratch it pays to buy the very best, even if you have to take out a bank loan to do so. The initial outlay may be more on top-grade pots and pans made, say, from stainless steel. But, being more heat-efficient they will be more economic with your fuel, and they will last longer.

Don't make the mistake, however, of buying very large pans

and casseroles in cast iron unless you have the muscles of a navvy. They may look very smart but once filled with food they can be amazingly heavy to handle.

Look out for auction or clearance sales of caterer's equipment, particularly when a restaurant closes down. If you're planning to do catering on a large scale, look out for things like hot cupboards to keep food warm, bain maries to do the same job in a different way, and thermostatically controlled deep fat fryers – some of them are small enough to sit on a table top.

You'll also need a food processor. If you're starting from scratch buy a family-sized one; not only do they take larger quantities but they have a more robust motor. Many small things of course can make your life easier, and the job faster too. Electric gadgets like a lemon squeezer, herb mill, carving knife may not be vital, but they make life easier for a busy cook. If you are making preserves or confectionery you may find also that you cannot do without a sugar thermometer, or a double pan for sauces and melting things like chocolate. If you are installing a new sink, a waste disposal unit would also help with the refuse problem.

Don't forget that you will inevitably have extra laundry to cope with: tea towels, overalls, oven gloves, plus, perhaps, table cloths and table napkins if you are catering for other people. Look out for old-fashioned white damask cloths at house sales. Incidentally, they can often be picked up at bargain prices since they are too large for ordinary domestic use.

You may have to re-think your freezer capacity. But before you rush out and buy the largest freezer you can find, remember one point: it is illegal to cook food, freeze it, then thaw it for re-sale. What you can do, however, is to freeze the components of, say, pies, in their uncooked state, that is, meat ready chopped, pastry dough made. Remember to take out insurance, too, in case your freezer breaks down or there is an electricity cut. Losing the contents is annoying enough for an average family; for a professional cook it could be a disaster.

BUYING YOUR PRODUCE

The caterer's best friend is the local cash and carry. If you don't know where yours is, ask a friendly café owner. You will probably have to get a registration card from them in order to buy, and this probably means producing at least a bank reference. However the cash and carry is not the only place to go. Keep an eagle eye open for really good offers in your local supermarket and load your trolley up with special offer non-perishable items like cut-price sugar.

If you're anywhere near the country, keep an eye on farm shops. Some of them, alas, are not as cheap as they would like you to believe. But if you need fresh produce for occasions such as dinner party catering, it pays to make friends with farmers. You can usually buy meat, too, in bulk at knock-down prices from these outlets. Pick-your-own places are good, too, especially if you are planning to make preserves. Rope in the family to help with the harvesting.

WHAT ARE YOU GOING TO COOK?

The world of cookery seems to be divided into people who like making soups, stews and savouries and those who prefer making cakes, sweets and biscuits. Then there is the lunatic fringe, like me, who are mad about making preserves. The chances are that *you* have a speciality cooking skill – is this the one that you are going to capitalise on? Before you decide, you need to ask yourself some questions:

Do I want to make the same thing every day?
You might find yourself doing this if you make things in batches for local food shops, tea-rooms, or making up sandwiches for the office trade. Don't entertain any ideas about making up food in bulk, then taking it to a friend to pack – that would contravene the regulations.

How much time do I have to spare, and when?

This will dictate whether you cook meals for other people in your home, then deliver them, or in fact, produce anything that has to be eaten right away. The time that you can spare may well be hedged around by responsibilities like having to fetch the children from school, or having an evening meal ready for the family.

Who are my potential customers?

There is little point in running a business doing fancy dinner parties, if you live in the middle of an industrial estate; or children's birthday cakes in a retirement area. Look around you and see who is likely to need your services, and what their tastes are.

Do I mind cooking in front of other people?

If you are the type that gets flustered when other people come into your kitchen when you're cooking, then rule out any idea of giving cookery classes, or preparing food then finishing it on the customer's premises. Instead, go for items you can cook, then sell in a ready-cooked state to shops or market stalls.

Can I handle problems calmly?

If you are going to specialise in outside catering, there's always going to be the time when there's a power cut when you're in the middle of cooking, someone drops a tray of canapés at a cocktail party, or you arrive with *boeuf en croûte* for a special lunch and find one of the guests is a strict vegetarian. In these situations you need to think quickly, carry on with a smile, and never let your customers know of the panic going on behind the scenes.

You may not come up against the extremes that I have in the catering business. We were running an Arab restaurant in Weybridge – I was fashion and beauty editor of *Good Housekeeping* by day, waitress at night. My husband phoned me at the office, 'Can you get home early tonight?' 'Why?' 'Because the chef has just been arrested by the local CID and you're going to have to do the cooking!'

Am I aware of current fashions in food?

If you are going to set up as a private cook, preparing meals for other people, you should set aside Elizabeth David and Delia Smith from time to time, and see what people are eating in the world outside, whether it's Tex Mex, Balti curries, gravad lax or stir-fries. At one time, for instance, the cheesecake was king. Then we had the great Kiwi fruit invasion, and I'm old enough to remember the year of the Black Forest gâteau.

Keep an eye on what people are raving about in the restaurants, read the cookery columns (and the restaurant critics' columns) to spot the trends and bone up on the recipes to be prepared.

Would I mind working in an onion or vinegar laden atmosphere all day, or having a house that smells of fish?

Chutney making, even on a small scale, gives the atmosphere a pungent pickle smell which lingers for hours. The same goes for things like onions, spicy foods and fish. Bear this in mind if you and your family have sensitive nostrils.

Do I have something special to offer?

If you're an expert on Vietnamese cooking, if your Austrian *apfel strudels* are raved over, then you have something to offer that the large professional catering companies cannot compete with. Capitalise on it.

Do I mind working unsocial hours?

If you are going in for outside catering, even if you are making the meals at home, be prepared for washing up at midnight, or getting up at dawn to prepare a picnic for twenty. Some cooks find the sheer variety and the uncertain hours a great stimulus. Others, with small children and a domestic routine to stick to, do not.

Am I strong and fit?

Cooking en masse involves a great deal of heavy lifting and lugging around of loaded trays, saucepans full of boiling water, perhaps cartons of wine. Don't go for this type of work if you think your physique won't stand up to it. Stick to something smaller scale.

SELLING YOURSELF AND YOUR PRODUCTS

It's no good hiding behind the gas stove, and waiting for the world to come to you. As a professional cook you're going to need to learn to sell your services one way or another. If you shy from promoting yourself, however, it's perfectly possible to start small as a professional cook, with favourite foods that your friends have always admired. You can sell your products in a small way via Women's Institute markets at first, then small restaurants, local food shops (many chic London shops rely on gifted local housewives for their quiches and other cooked foods), before going on to more complicated agendas like catering for dinner parties.

Presentation

Whatever you do, presentation is the name of the game. Your pies or jams may taste delicious, but they have to look good, too. And you can learn a lot about this subject simply by strolling round specialist food departments in smart stores like Harrods, Fortnum and Mason, or your local specialist delicatessen, to see how other people have packaged their wares. Small cakes need to be presented in decorative paper cases for instance. And it's simple to make attractive covers for jam and pickle jars from pieces of check gingham cut into circles with pinking shears, for a home made look. Then add your own 'designer' labels, which are hand written and then photostated – you could even learn simple italic writing for this purpose.

CATERING FOR OTHERS

This kind of cookery falls into two natural categories: special celebration meals, possibly buffets; and smaller, regular ones, backing up local hostesses who entertain a great deal. It pays to prepare most of the food in your own kitchen, using familiar equipment, and then just finish it off at the client's home. Going into an unfamiliar setting, and searching for vital tools at the last moment can cause stress, so always take a basic 'surgeon's kit' of things like knives, slotted spoons, a garlic press, tin-opener and corkscrew with you.

Lunch and dinner parties

Whether it's a small dinner party or a banquet you have to cater for, it's vital that you spend time with your customers beforehand, finding out exactly what the scene is likely to be. So have a list of pertinent questions ready:

How many guests are expected?
And is the figure likely to be a firm one? Always bear in mind that there may be an extra couple at the last minute, or somebody may pull out. It's a good idea to make it clear to the customer that the charge remains the same if anyone pulls out within, say 24 hours of the event.) So it's best to buy the raw ingredients as near as possible to the actual date, unless you can use up any spare food without eating into your profits. If the numbers are large and the space cramped, it might be tactful to suggest a buffet party rather than a sit-down meal.

Are there going to be late arrivals?
And are guests likely to run over time with their pre-dinner drinks? In that case, anything like a soufflé, that needs finishing at the last minute for the first course, could cause problems. It's safer to start with something cold. It would also be wise to have casseroled rather than fried food for the main course so that it cannot be spoilt.

Are they likely to linger over their meal?

If there are likely to be speeches, if a great deal of drink is being served or a lot of animated conversations are expected, then the meal could drag on for a long time. This means that last-minute hot puddings are not a good idea. You'll need to have something cold but exotic that's been prepared beforehand.

Are you expected to serve the food – or disappear?

A friend of mine makes a good living as a 'ghost' chef. She provides complete dinner parties for people who pretend they have cooked the meal themselves. I once delivered a fabulous four-course meal for her to the back door of the house of a woman who was famed locally for her dinners. I had strict instructions to arrive and depart well before the first guests appeared. And besides the food, I also had to give a detailed list of what was in everything, and how it was prepared – just in case the hostess was quizzed about it!

Who's providing the drink?

Always be prepared to give your hostess recommendations for appropriate wine to serve with the meal. If you're expected to provide the drinks, then ask for money in advance as they can be an expensive item. Add a mark-up for your trouble: restaurants double the price of most of the wine they serve, but you don't need to go that far!

Is the hostess rich, or hard up?

Try to gauge in advance how much your customer is going to be prepared to spend. There's no point in working on an up-market menu for her, heavy on smoked salmon, game and similarly expensive items if she is short of cash. With a little ingenuity, and a lot of vegetables, you can spin out high-cost items like meat and still produce a mouth-watering, satisfying meal. Expensive fresh soft fruit – raspberries out of season for instance – goes a long way when spun out in a tart, or whipped with crème fraîche and a dash of brandy.

Are there other services you can sell?
With the right back-up team of enthusiastic home workers like
yourself, you could offer flower arrangements, music, and a
take you home taxi service – and take a cut. You could gradually
build yourself up, this way, as a party organizer.

Finger food

There's money to be made from making tempting foods that
don't need the services of a knife and fork. At one end of the
scale you could specialise in imaginative cocktail canapés, even
doing a trade in frozen food with them. At the other, you could
be producing a 'finger' buffet for a large number of people,
serving things on bases made from pastry, bread or, more
fashionably, pizza dough.

People will patronise you for this kind of food because they
know that it is fiddly and time-consuming to make it themselves.
However, that should make alarm bells ring in your head as far
as costings are concerned. These items will take longer to get
together than anything else you are likely to cook, not just in the
processing but in the large number of ingredients to be bought.
So be meticulous in your figures, make sure you have allowed
enough for your time. Having got your sums right, however,
you are on to a winning product, for small amounts of quite
exotic ingredients can be stretched a long way, and the perceived value of the product is bound to be high.

The sandwich scene

Supplying sandwiches to local office staff can be a lucrative
business if you get your fillings right, and if they are hygienically
wrapped to conform with the food regulations.

Be inventive with your ideas; study the market. If you're
selling to an all-girl office you would probably tend to do best by
majoring heavily on 'diet' sandwiches with low-calorie fillings,
or perhaps individual salads, while men are likely to want
something more hearty. This is rapidly becoming an over-
crowded market, so do your research first. A brand new office

block may not yet have been tackled by a rival sandwich-maker and you may have a chance to get in first! And don't forget people like hairdressers, who find it difficult to nip out to buy sandwiches between crowded appointments. You might be able to supply their clients, too. If you can find your customers, snacks and sandwiches can provide a good regular income. But be prepared to get up at dawn to start your sandwich-making! It's a good idea to rehearse your sandwich making to see how certain fillings react to waiting an hour or so before being eaten. You will need plenty of fridge space for storing.

HOME BAKING

Cakes and biscuits are attractive things to make, and give you a chance to show off your artistic talent in the way you decorate them. If you have a flair for this kind of cookery, your customers could include the local tea-rooms as well as private customers who want something special for a party or a wedding. Remember that small items like scones, buns, fairy cakes and biscuits fetch more money than one large item that has to be sliced, unless it is a party cake.

Breads

Steer clear of selling conventional home-made bread, even if your loaves rise to perfection, because you will land yourself in a weights and measures jungle. However, malt loaves, fruit loaves and those with nuts and/or cheese in them don't come under this heading and are well worth making. You could, for instance keep away from the baguette but do some of the traditional French country breads, those containing olives or nuts. However, you will need to give the weight of the loaf, so weigh the ingredients meticulously and make some samples until you are confident that you can turn out the same size loaves each time.

If you're planning a cake-making company, first research the supermarkets and bakers to see what is already on sale in packaged form. You will have great difficulty in persuading people that your jam turnovers really do taste good and not like cardboard, as so many of the packaged ones do.

Go for tradition instead. Find old recipes – search through Mrs Beeton and other heritage cookbooks for them – and make something with a story to it. Local regional specialities like lardy cake, parkin, old maids, and Eccles cakes are obvious choices. If you package them attractively they might sell to tourists, too. And don't feel that lardy cakes have to be cooked in Wiltshire, they might appreciate them in the north. Oven space is going to be at a premium, so go for rectangular rather than round tins; then you'll be able to fit more cakes in at one time.

Selling from stalls

A good way to get into the home baking trade is to sell at a Women's Institute market (see Help Section, page 191 for further details). Your first time at the market, take a mix of things and see which items go quickly, then concentrate on those. If you have something really unusual, however, give it a fair trial – say a month – in the hope that it catches on; but do it in small batches. If your cakes have a story of any kind, tell it – write out an informative card for people to read. You will find the local market organiser will be a great help to you on things like pricing.

COOKING FOR RESTAURANTS, WINE BARS, PUBS

Although chefs are now emerging as the true stars of the restaurant business, and running their own establishments, it's a fact of life that wine bars and pubs are staffed on the whole by non-cooks.

They rely heavily on pre-prepared food that can be micro-waved at the last moment – and that is where you could come in. For the managers of many of these outlets would be relieved to have an outside cook who could be relied upon to deliver the goods, especially if they had a 'home-made' air to them. Steer clear of those two wine-bar standbys, chilli con carne and quiche. But offer them real home-cooked soups, for instance, and you would be an immediate hit.

You could also offer unusual pies, tarts, and desserts other than the mass-produced cardboard-tasting variety that are usually served up. If they wanted to give the impression, at least, that they were producing the food themselves, you could supply it ready for last-minute finishing – a pie, perhaps with a pastry lid on top that could be cooked at the last minute, emerging crisp and golden from the oven. Ready-made salad mixes like tuna with green beans, coronation chicken, home-made pâtés such as chicken liver or kipper, would be appreciated by pubs for the lunch-time trade.

Top-class restaurants are unlikely to need your services, but aspiring ones down the scale might well be interested in unusual breads to serve with the cheese course, super desserts which the chef can pass off as his own and, if they are really into new food, the top chef's latest toy, *amuse-gueules*, the pre-dinner equiv-alent of petits fours, tiny pastries and pieces of toasted bread spread with things like tapenade, or confiture of onion. Although tiresome and time-consuming for a busy chef, these would be easy to make and decorate from home, and deliver to the back door.

PRESERVES, PICKLES AND CHUTNEYS

Use the fruits of summer to make unusual pickles and preserves for profit, using fruits from your garden or pick-your-own fruit farms. Don't just think in terms of putting your products in specialist grocer's shops. You could sell to restaurants and tea-rooms who would be happy not only to use the product but sell your jars for you at the cash desk. Market stalls and car boot sales are another outlet. And, once you grow in confidence, there are all sorts of possibilities, selling through the post for instance, taking small-ads to do so. Indeed, you could eventually build up a small catalogue, including Christmas hampers of your products as gift items.

As we all know, A is for additives, and there are strict rules over what you can and can't add to your product to enhance it. Some additives are used as colourants, others as preservatives. Get an up-to-date manual on the subject before you use any, and be sure you mention them among the ingredients on the label.

A pickle-maker's best friend is her freezer. This is one case where that particular piece of equipment comes into its own. For you can buy fruit and vegetables at glut times and literally put them on ice until you are ready to use them. Unless you have a stove with a simmering oven, as an Aga does, you'll also need a boiler to sterilise your jars. Hygiene is vitally important in making preserves for sale. It would be embarrassing to be summoned to collect a batch of jars with mould growing on the top of the jam. And you would lose rather than make money.

If you are making preserves you'll need to comply with the regulations regarding labelling. You're perfectly free to give your jars a home-made look with a label that says Old Mother Evans's Strawberry Jam in crabby handwriting. But somewhere on the jar there must be the following information: A list of ingredients (in order of weight), a 'best before' or 'use by' rating and any special condition of storage or use, such as: 'Once opened, store in a refrigerator.' Your name and address must be given (this could be good for future sales) and a lot or batch mark. These could all be put on to a separate small printed label on the back.

If you grow your own herbs, don't forget that herb vinegars are very profitable and easy to make, and you could also try herb mustards, pounding them into bought-in French English or German mustard, then re-potting them.

SWEETS AND CONFECTIONERY

Home-made sweets of all kinds are always considered a good buy, especially if you pack them attractively. If you have a repertoire of sweet recipes up your sleeve, from home-made toffee to Turkish delight or peppermint creams, then cash in on them – they may well make you a fortune. Elizabeth Shaw, of chocolate peppermint cream fame, started her business off in a kitchen, as did several other successful confectioners who have long since successfully sold out to big concerns – and pocketed the cash.

Working with chocolate – making hand-made truffles, chocolates and even Easter eggs is a skill that can be learned, and it is easy to buy moulds for the purpose. Petits fours, made from moulded marzipan are also easy to concoct, and you can then top them with nuts, hundreds and thousands, or other decorations. To be successful with these you need a regular contract with, say a restaurant, as they deteriorate quickly.

Crystallised fruits are another form of confectionery that is fun, especially if you grow your own angelica, violets, rose petals. These will keep for some time if they are properly packed and could realise good profits, especially at Christmas time. All confectionery needs to be attractively presented, so your initial outlay will have to include things like cellophane bags, perhaps luxury cardboard boxes with see-through tops. The local tearooms or sweet shop might take loose candies from you, but most people will want them boxed or bagged.

SPECIAL OCCASION FOOD

If you are planning to tap into the world of party catering, then you must have an attractive brochure listing your services, with sample menus. And, if possible you should also have an album of photographs of party food you have done, so the would-be client will get an idea of your skills.

If you are covering a celebration of some kind which might involve hiring cutlery and glass, gilt chairs, even a marquee, this is a chance for you to make some more money out of the deal. Check out reliable suppliers (start off in the *Yellow Pages*) and then offer to take the chore off your hostess's hands. Once you've established such contacts, keep a note of them in your address book so that next time you have all the details at your fingertips.

Weddings and christenings

Whether you offer the whole catering package or just the cake depends on the scope of your business and how long you have been operating as a catering company. You need quite a lot of expertise to cost out a wedding breakfast or a christening party, and unless you are sure of your figures you could end up in effect by paying your customer for the privilege of doing it, rather than being paid. On the other hand, if you are secure in your costings, harassed parents are always looking for someone reliable to cater for events like these at a reasonable price.

Cakes, on the other hand are always well worth doing since they are perceived to be of high value. If cake decorating is your particular talent, then this is definitely an area where you can make money.

Fun cakes

A business making fun birthday and other anniversary cakes, perhaps delivered as a surprise like a kissogram but more appreciated – should go well in any highly populated area. Consider the possibility of delivering to offices, for instance. In the large organisations for which I have worked, any member of staff who has a birthday is obliged to trot out a cake in good time for the afternoon tea-break, and that's where you could come in, doing something themed. I've never seen a cake in the shape of a computer yet, but no doubt it has been done!

To do special occasion cakes you need more than the talent to turn out something spectacular, you also have to like dealing with people. You need to chat to prospective customers about their life-style, their hobbies – gleaning all the background information you can before coming up with a cake design. You should have an album of your work, not only so they can see how good you are, but also to spark off ideas. If you are just starting, then make up some fancy cakes and photograph them, imply they were for other customers without actually saying so! Sell the cakes to your local *pâtisserie*.

Show the customers actual samples of icing colours (spread on strips of cardboard) so that when you are talking about green or blue they know what they're going to get. And be sure to find out at the start how much they are thinking of paying for the finished product.

When you're designing a cake, bear in mind that you will probably also have to deliver it, and one that is made up of components that are iced together on the spot is more likely to survive the journey than a leaning tower of Pisa in a box in the back of the car. Save items like polystyrene chips to help with the packaging, and don't use packaging such as plastic bags that might adhere to the surface and spoil the icing.

Children's party packages

Many harassed mothers, especially those in full-time jobs, would be delighted to hear of someone who could deliver an entire birthday party for a child. Tastes in party food have changed over the years, and things like jelly and cream cakes are currently out of favour, being replaced by sausage rolls, mini-pizzas and tiny hamburgers on sticks, so get a very clear idea of not only what your hostess but also the child in question is expecting in the way of food.

Suggest themes to them – Ninja turtles, pirates, dinosaurs, anything that is currently on the TV screens (see what the latest offerings from Disney are) and come up with some ideas for a party tea on those lines. If you have a well-developed entrepre-neurial streak you could offer to supply paper cups, napkins, streamers, even small cheap presents for the guests as well, and take the whole thing off the parent's hands. Extra services like this would bring in much more cash than simply making a party cake, and get you talked about in the neighbourhood as somebody worth patronising in the future. Assemble a list of conjurers, clowns, and other entertainers (look at small ads in your local paper or free sheet) and you could find yourself running a business as a fully-fledged party organiser.

Club events

If you like doing large-scale catering, then look out for the opportunity to do special events for local clubs and societies. Cricket club teas, originally the province of cricketing wives, may well be up for grabs as busy women are no longer keen to work this way at weekends. If your local club is running out of volunteers, and your price is right, they might well be interested in hiring you. If you're catering for any sporting event, by the way, go for large quantities and hearty food since you'll be dealing with large appetites!

OTHER WAYS OF WORKING WITH FOOD

Foreign food

As we have become more cosmopolitan in our eating habits, more and more of us are serving so-called 'ethnic' foods at parties. And if your background is, say, Chinese, Indian or Italian, you have a heritage to cash in on for special occasion events. You could offer a wider and more interesting range of foods than the local restaurants, and attractive serving dishes that are in keeping with them. Advertise your services in a local paper, and try to get an article written about you in the local press, too (phone the women's page editor). Or write an article about yourself, how you set up your business, what you offer, and send it to your local paper or free sheet.

Food for photography and films

Cooking for photography and filming is a highly specialised job. But if you have worked as a home economist, the chances are that you have been involved in this kind of activity. The emphasis now is on 'real' food for magazine pictures – the days when shaving cream was used instead of meringue for instance are almost over. However there are still some tricks in the trade – like stuffing a 'steak and kidney pie' with crumpled newspaper instead of meat, and painting oil over the surface of other dishes so that they gleam attractively.

If this kind of specialised, but very well paid catering appeals to you, then the best way to learn is to apprentice yourself to someone who is already doing this work.

Claude, a former fashion model, now specialises in making food for TV. 'I used to do the odd commercial and that's how I got in. I invited some of the team back for a meal, they admired my food, and the producer asked me if I would do the catering for a commercial they were shooting. It's exhausting but fun. The worst thing that happened to me was when my car was in a crash, and all the food went on the floor!'

Marese, on the other hand, is the behind-the-scenes help for a programme fronted by a cooking celebrity. 'You probably think that she prepares the finished dishes herself,' says Marese, who is a trained home economist. 'In actual fact she's far too busy – and that's where I come in.'

Food styling is another off-shoot of the photographic scene. People are hired to find exactly the right table settings, dishes and background accessories to complement the scene. If you have had experience working on a magazine or for a photographer, this could be an option.

Writing cook books

It has to be said straight away that the cookery book market is already well served with authors. But if you have a completely innovative idea for a cookery book, then it might be worthwhile contacting a publisher. Or you could try selling a cookery column to your local newspaper – if it hasn't got one already.

If you have had some publishing experience, then it is possible you might find work proof reading cookery recipes – which is something that requires a very accurate mind plus basic cooking skills.

Hiring out equipment

If you are cooking on a large scale, the chances are that you'll have soon stocked up with a considerable amount of crockery and glassware. A useful side-line to a catering business is the hire of china and glasses for special occasions. Advertise your services in the local paper; make sure you get a deposit for break-ages. Some hiring services ask their clients **not** to wash up glassware after use. You can choose whether or not to do so, but if it is returned to you that way, remember to cost in more for the use of your dishwasher.

THE SOCIAL COOK

If you're a good cook, like people, and have a bulging address book, then the professional dinner party is a way of making friends and money at the same time. You announce to your mailing list (acquired via contacts and friends) that you are giving a themed dinner party on such and such a date (e.g. French, Mexican or Italian evening) and the price of an invitation will be so much. Your reputation will spread rapidly via personal recommendations and your guests will come, not only for the food, but to meet new friends.

Louise, an energetic American, runs regular dinner parties that are highly successful. 'I had the idea back in the States in the 1980s,' she says. 'I had been ill with glandular fever and away from my job, so I had time to do a lot of thinking. I assessed the situation and realised that the two things I liked doing best were cooking and giving parties. I'd heard of another American who was running a private supper club in Paris, so when I moved to London I thought I would try the idea myself.' At first Louise entertained once a month as a spare-time project. After a while she decided to give up her job and run her parties full-time.

Every Friday, twenty or more people converge on her large London flat around 7.30 pm, for aperitifs served in her living room. Then at 8.30 pm, they sit down to dine. As they arrive, Louise makes a particular point of asking her guests about themselves, then introduces them to a clutch of people. At most parties she has a friend (who eats free), who takes over this task when she needs to disappear into the kitchen.

Because of the numbers involved, Louise sets a series of separate tables, all with flower arrangements, candles and place names. There are copies of the menu on each table.

The diners are an ever-changing mélange: some are regulars, others newcomers brought by friends. As Louise used to work in theatre design circles, many of them come from the arts, and include a fascinating mix of nationalities. The seating plans have to be worked out particularly carefully so that, as well as eating good food, people who come for the evening know that they are going to meet fellow guests who are compatible and interesting. She has to take note, too, of guests' special needs. 'What I really loathe', says Louise, 'is getting a vegan – they are almost impossible to cater for and have to have special dishes to themselves. The evenings are usually themed, and recently Louise has been featuring different regions of France, something that has proved particularly popular.

As hostess as well as cook, Louise has to plan ahead. 'It's very important to be totally organised,' she says. 'I plan a menu that includes a number of things that can be prepared the day before – perhaps a starter and/or a dessert. I've had to buy a giant refrigerator to store the food, but it's proved worth-while.' Now she has a young student to help behind the scenes with serving and last minute cooking chores. Strictly speaking, she should have a licence to serve wine, and is thinking of applying for one. 'At the moment however, I simply charge for the meal, and throw in the drink free – that way I don't contravene the law!'

COSTINGS, INSURANCE AND TRANSPORT

Costing

Food costing can be really tricky – the price of the basic ingredients fluctuate for one thing, and estimating just how much a given number of people will eat takes practice, especially when you are dealing with something like a buffet party.

If you are batch baking, basically you have to add up the cost of the ingredients, plus your time, plus the cost of packaging, delivery, and overheads such as electricity. This will give you the amount it costs you. What you charge the customer will depend on where you live (prices are always higher in a city), what local people are used to paying for a similar product, and a reasonable return on your hard work.

If you are catering for other people, then costing is trickier. First let your fingers do the walking – look in the *Yellow Pages* for rival firms to the one you are aiming to set up, and get estimates from them for a non-existent occasion. You can then just under-cut their price. Don't feel too bad about it – one day someone will do the same to you!

You will also have to scale up your basic recipes accurately. Judy Ridgeway, in her book *Running Your Own Catering Company* (see Help Section, page 191) says that the trick is to convert all the ingredients of a recipe into weights (for example, a white of egg averages 25g). Then convert, say, a recipe for four people to quantities for 40 by multiplying by ten. Do your own portion control by serving food in ready-cut portions wherever possible. If you are doing a buffet, it is lethal to set out gateaux, then leave the diners to cut their own slices!

Amateurs often make the mistake of pricing their produce so low that people are unable to resist the bargain. The problem is that it is much easier to come down on your prices than to raise them – people become suspicious if you do. So try to get your prices right at the beginning. If you are selling at a place like a Women's Institute market, the organisers will help you.

Insurance

Anyone running a catering business needs good insurance back-up. Apart from covering events like power cuts which could affect the cooker, the fridge and freezer, you'll need cover against accidental food poisoning and, if you are catering for other people, breakages to their crockery, or yours etc. (See the Help Section, page 181 for further information on insurance.)

Transport

As you will almost certainly be ferrying food around, consider the car at your disposal. Regulations say, not unreasonably, that the same vehicle must not be used for conveying food and animals, so if the family pet has to be taken anywhere it will have to be in another vehicle. You need a car with a roomy boot (later, if you do well, you may want to invest in a van with racks in it). A hatchback is the best choice as when the rear door is shut your food is hidden from would-be thieves by the parcel shelf. Check with your local Environmental Health officer to find out what the local requirements are for transporting food by car.

Business Ideas

*Book-keeping ... Accommodation address ...
Faxing and photostatting, Typing, Stationery
design ... Translating ... Telephone answering,
Computer services ... Selling insurance ...
Networking ... Party selling ... Telephone selling
... Market research ... Search services ... Proof
reading and indexing ... Hiring out ... Hiring at
home ... Outworking ... Laundry services ...
Agencies ... Selling pictures and antiques ...
Creative writing ... Freelance journalism ... Travel
writing ... Photography ... Running a picture
library ... Astrology ... Graphology ... Tarot ... I
Ching ... Runes ... Biorhythms*

SETTING UP A BUSINESS in your home is easy, and starting it should not involve you in a high outlay. There are any number of jobs you can do, simply armed with a desk and a telephone – you'll find suggestions on the following pages.

Many professional services could easily be switched from office to home. As a solicitor, for instance, it would be perfectly possible for you to set up a home-based practice. And anyone who has trained in accountancy would have no difficulty in working from home, building up a personal clientele, undercutting other accountancy firms and perhaps specialising in, say, farmers, writers, builders, or any group of people with particular tax concerns. Accountants, like solicitors, usually charge for their time by the hour, and by the letter written on the client's behalf.

Even if you are not qualified to do professional work, there are all sorts of services that you could offer the business world.

OFFICE SERVICES

Book-keeping

If you are basically numerate and accurate, book-keeping for small businessmen is not a difficult skill to learn. Local business colleges or evening institutes run classes in the subject and you can buy text books too, setting it all out. As with accountancy, you could specialise in a particular set of people, taking their books home weekly or monthly to keep them up to date.

Doing VAT returns would be part of your duties – indeed you could probably make some useful cash just specialising in those. All you need for the task, basically, is a calculator, a telephone, a note of the latest tax regulations, and a good head for figures. But if you have a computer and can offer to run off spread sheets, cash flow forecasts, accounts so much the better.

Accommodation address

Many people need an accommodation address for varying reasons. This is something you could provide. People who live abroad or move around a great deal, might well like to have their letters sent to you. If you live in London or any big city, many small country-based firms might be glad to use your services. Decide whether you are going to simply keep their mail for them or forward it on, and charge accordingly. Either way, the work is not onerous. But it's essential for your own peace of mind that you are happy with the businesses you're representing. Avoid anything with the least suspicion of seediness about it. Get personal references if you're not sure.

Faxing and photostatting

If you already have or are thinking of investing in a fax and/or a photostat machine – these now come in table-top models – you could offer a service to local people, undercutting the professionals in the high street. I was astounded recently, when my own fax broke down, to find the high prices charged for the service by a little corner shop. Both these types of machines have come down dramatically in price recently, as more and more of us have them in our homes. If you wanted to make your service even more personal you could collect and deliver work on a regular basis.

Typing

If you're a competent, accurate typist, preparing manuscripts for authors and academics is both interesting and profitable. If you own a word processor with a spelling-check facility, rather than a typewriter, better still, since your work will look even more professional and be done much more speedily.

To find customers, try advertising in the local paper, and in the *Writers' and Artists' Yearbook*. Also contact The Society of Authors and The Writers' Guild of Great Britain (see Help Section, page 192). If you give a speedy, accurate service, your name will soon get passed on by word of mouth. It's worth while contacting universities and colleges too, to offer a service typing students' theses. Remember also that professional people like solicitors or barristers would be glad to hear about you, in case they want something done in an emergency and there is no one available in the office.

If you have a computer or an electronic typewriter (if you haven't, consider investing in one) then you can give your customers the extra service of a choice of type-faces. Make up a specimen sheet so that they can choose for themselves. Enquire, discreetly, whether you are allowed to correct their grammar or spelling if necessary – some people are weak in either or both areas and would welcome such a service.

Typing is usually charged out by the page or per thousand words. If you have to set it out specially (say, with inset blocks of different type faces), then you should charge more. If the handwriting is bad, or the original manuscript is heavily corrected, then it is best to charge by the hour. And don't forget to add in the cost of the paper itself, plus things like photostats, or extra print-outs.

Preparing CVs

Preparing or up-dating CVs (curricula vitae) is another special-ised off-shoot of the typing business that you might consider. Many young professional people move around a great deal in the initial stages of their careers and need to keep their CVs up to date. Contact local colleges, hospitals and other likely insti-tutions and offer your services.

Deadlines are essential in this kind of work, and you can reckon on being handed material at the very last minute, so be prepared to work overnight if necessary, and charge accord-ingly. Build up a reputation for being both fast and accurate, however, and you can't go wrong.

You could also get regular work from a typing agency. This means that you have to keep yourself free at all times to accept work, otherwise they are not likely to use you twice. Look in your local paper or specialist magazines for the names of firms who employ people for this work. You could also start a typing agency yourself, farming out work to other people, but if you set this up as a business you may need a licence (see Help Section, page 193). However, this could be a useful regular income for you.

Translating

If you have language skills it should be easy to find work at home translating letters, manuscripts, features from magazines, and books, or the even more specialised work of indexing in a foreign language. If you have, say a specialist technical know-ledge of medical or other scientific words then you can charge more than the going rate for this work. It is normal, by the way, to translate from the foreign language into English, not vice versa, unless you are a foreign national.

Get your name on the lists of public libraries, and academic establishments, approach local firms who you know have regu-lar contacts abroad, or foreign firms coming into your area. You could also join the Institute of Linguists or the Translators' Association which deals mainly with publishing (see Help Section 192).

There is also a lucrative income to be made from helping foreigners to compose difficult or official letters in English. If you have access to a local ethnic community, it would be worth while offering your services. You could also bolster your income by giving language lessons, either in conversation or perhaps to school children, or to students who need extra help before their exams (see Section Seven page 163). It may be, too, that local firms could do with your services occasionally as an interpreter.

Translating is normally paid per page or thousand words, but if you are faced with something like an index or a list, then you should charge by the hour for your work. Join the Institute of Linguists (see Help Section, page 192); they will advise you on current rates for the job.

Telephone answering

If you've a good 'telephone voice', and are prepared to stay home during office hours, you could earn useful extra cash by taking telephone messages for people. More personal and flexible than an answering machine, your service would be welcomed by many harrassed local professional people whose work depends on their being out and about all the time. They could keep in constant contact with you to check out their messages or you could refer callers to another number for them. Advertise your services in the local paper.

Computer Services

If you own a computer and can work it competently you have a whole spectrum of opportunities before you, whether it is doing spread sheets of figures for small firms, typing manuscripts for authors, even desk-top publishing of leaflets, booklets.

Starting from scratch

You may be thinking of buying and using a computer for the first time and setting yourself up in business. In that case, don't suffer from the same delusion as many people I've met. They are under the impression that the machine does all the work for you, and all you have to do is to sit back and press keys! Remember, someone has to put the text and information into the computer in the first place. And that someone is you! So if you are a beginner, there is a great deal of learning and then inputting to be done.

Make sure that you buy the right machine for your eventual needs. The cheaper models are fine for would-be authors, for writing letters, or doing the odd account. But if you are venturing into doing complicated spread sheets or desk-top publishing you will need something more powerful and versatile. All computers, on the face of it, overlap in what they can offer. The difference between the cheap ones and the more expensive ones is the amount of work you have to put in. The more expensive machines are faster to use, and often more idiot proof (mine says 'Do you **really** want to throw this file away?' for instance). As so many offices are constantly up-dating their machines and dumping the old ones, it may pay you to invest in a second hand version of an expensive machine rather than a new cheap one.

If, on the other hand, you are experienced in this work, there are all sorts of outlets you could try. Not least of these is teaching other people how to use their machine. Some of the worst, most incomprehensible instruction books in the world come with the most popular brands of computer. Text-books are little better. So anyone who can show new owners *simply*, stage by stage, how to use their Amstrad or Macintosh is bound to find people willing to pay for that service.

The software you choose is vital. Depending on what you are doing, you may need things like a dictionary, spelling check, word count and so on. If you are planning to do outside work for a particular company then you might need a machine which is compatible with theirs, so that floppy disks can be sent to them rather than printed out pages.

If you are using a word processor for your professional work, then you will need to invest in something other than the basic dot matrix printer. Both laser and ink-jet printers, which give a professional 'printed' look, are coming down rapidly in price, and you may be able to pick up one second-hand which would be even cheaper.

Designing letter-heads

If you have a computer with a word-processing software, it is easy to learn how to design letter-heads for people with the range of type faces and sizes at your disposal. Fully fledged graphic design firms charge a great deal of money for this work, so you could easily undercut them and still make money.

SELLING

Insurance

Good money can be had from selling insurance, whether you act as an agent for a particular company, or, better still, you go on to become a broker. The commission the companies pay is high but, at the same time, if your customer decides to give up their insurance cover, you may be asked to pay some of it back. You need very little training except in the 'product' that you are going to sell, since the company concerned will back you up with quotations and estimates. You do, however, have to be good at handling people.

It pays to have a list of contacts to begin with but it is not always necessary. William makes a good living from home by selling insurance to aspiring executives in a large local company. 'I've made friends with the receptionist there, and she gives me a copy of the company magazine so I know who has just been promoted or had a special birthday or won an award,' says William. 'I then ring them up and congratulate them – and go on to sell from there.'

Patricia started selling insurance from home because she decided she was 'unemployable'. 'I can't work for people who are less intelligent than me,' she says. She saw an advertisement in a national newspaper for 'Ambitious people who would like to be self-employed'. She applied for the job, and was called for an interview by the insurance division of one of the big banks. They hired her on the spot.

'"Can you talk to strangers?" was one of the questions they asked,' says Patricia. 'They also wanted to assure themselves that I had earned a good salary in the past and done well in my previous job. They didn't want dead-beats.'

Training

She was sent to London for a week's training in product knowledge, followed by a week in Birmingham being taught how to sell. 'I was so naïve at that time that I was convinced I was selling some sort of investment project – it took me eighteen months to realise it was insurance!'

Then Patricia returned home and started 'cold calling' as it is known in the profession, that is, ringing up total strangers. 'It took me ten days to make my first sale,' she remembers. 'Basically, it's a numbers game – every time you get your sixth turn-down you know you should make a sale in the seventh.

'Selling insurance has taught me two things: start and finish work at a set time every day, even if you don't have anyone to call, and, on Friday afternoon, get all your book work up to date then take the weekend off.'

Patricia is really happy in her work. 'Being a woman helps, I think. I've always felt I am doing a first-class job. There are so many orphans and widows left poor because no provision has been made for them. Every time I sell a family life assurance I know that I have done them so much good. I've seen what happens when they don't have it, there is so much misery left behind.'

Networking

Multi-level, or network marketing – that is, selling goods from one particular company to the public on a regular basis – has come to us from the USA, where one in five millionaires are said to have made their money this way. It is now catching on fast in this country. And it is claimed that more than half a million people are now working from home in this way. This particular form of selling would appeal to anyone who wants to set up a business without having to pay large initial costs, an occupation where they can choose how many hours they put in.

It works this way: you become one of a network of distributors for a particular range of products – it could be concentrated detergent, cosmetics, skin care products, polishes – which your customers will buy on a regular basis. In addition to selling direct, you also get a bonus on goods sold by any new recruits you bring into the network. So, if you are energetic and successful, part of your income derives from work done by other people.

An up-dated form of the old method of pyramid selling, which was outlawed back in the 1970s, networking is operated by companies as widely different as the Kleeneze brush company, and Herbalife, the vitamin people and Amway who manufacture household cleaning products. The difference between pyramid selling and network marketing, which is governed by strict laws passed in 1973, is that in the former case you had to pay a large fee to join up, with networking you don't.

You need some capital, but you only buy as much stock as you can sell, at any time, and the law stops you from spending more than £75 in your first week of membership. Remember selling is the operative word. So if you don't like selling – particularly to friends and neighbours – you won't be happy in a networking organisation.

Tom and Janetta were attracted to networking as a way of getting some extra cash to prop up their garden nursery business in the low season. It works perfectly for them, as the peak time of selling coincides with the down-turn in work at the nursery: around Christmas time.

They spend around two months of the year on the business, selling mainly through presentations at their home to around half a dozen people at a time. They also make 'downline' money from the sales of new recruits to the organisation that they have sponsored. They are doing so well that they reckon they will be self-supporting from their networking sales within eighteen months.

Think things through carefully before committing yourself. Networking is not a 'get rich quick' scheme. You have to have a serious commitment, for it's not just a matter of sales, you also have to distribute the products and arrange presentations. The Department of Trade and Industry has guide-lines to help you distinguish between reputable firms and cowboys (see Help Section, page 192). But apart from checking out the firm, you need to make sure there is likely to be a continuing demand for their products in your area. Remember that, with the best will in the world, networking companies can go bankrupt so choose one with a well known reputation, and preferably with a long track record.

Party selling

The well known Tupperware was probably the first product to be sold in the home on a party plan. Now you can market jewellery, underwear, household goods, even sex aids that way. There are two ways of acting as a party organiser – you can either sell the goods with a fixed commission, usually around 20 per cent, or you can buy from the firm concerned, add your own mark-up and sell them at a price of your choice.

Once taken on as an organiser, you are usually given a short training course before you start giving selling parties in your home. You will then be expected to find other people to host parties at which you will demonstrate the products. Clearly an ability to get on well with people, and to sell, are vital requirements for this kind of work. You will also have to have somewhere to store the goods which will be delivered to you for distribution.

June has been holding selling parties at her home for some years now. 'I started off with jewellery, but found it was a bit slow except at times like Christmas, so I've now switched to nighties and underwear,' she says. 'I live on a big estate, and I don't have any difficulty finding customers – my friends really look forward to the parties. They think they are a riot.' June says that she makes enough money from her parties to take the family on a luxury holiday each year. But she reckons that if she wanted to work harder at it, she could make a reasonable regular income.

Points to watch with the party plan are that you take into account the cost of providing drinks and snacks for your customers, and that you check before signing up that the company concerned does not expect you to buy any 'promotional material' – a trick used by cowboy firms to get money out of you. Never hand over any of the clients' money until you have received the goods, and always have a separate bank account for these transactions.

Find party sales organisations by asking through friends, through small advertisements in the weekend national newspapers. Or, if you have a brand in mind, look them up in the phone book. Arrange to attend a party given for the product and see what you think of it before committing yourself.

Telephone selling

This kind of selling, which is relatively new to this country, is just one business enterprise that you can run from home. 'Cold calling', whether you are selling fitted kitchens or double glazing, is only for the bold. You have to be prepared to take rebuffs, so no shrinking violets need apply! You make the initial contact, then they send in a salesman or woman.

Some firms work on a commission basis, others pay by the call. Check them out carefully – you could be left with a horrendous telephone bill and no pay. Ask to speak to someone who is actually doing this job for them before committing yourself.

HOME SERVICES

Market Research

Not all market researchers stop people in the street to ask if they eat margarine – a lot of research is done over the telephone these days. There is also work to be done, processing the research data that companies receive. For more details contact the Market Research Society (see Help Section, page 193)

Search services

The good old *Yellow Pages* may be invaluable if you're looking for a particular service or product, but there are certain things that need a personal touch:

John, who had worked in a local bookshop for years, was devastated when it closed down and he was out of work.

'I was looking around for something to do to raise money, when I realised my house was stuffed full of books, most of them on music, many of which I had no use for. I decided to advertise them for sale in a specialist magazine, and found some buyers immediately.' John found that as a spin-off to this, two things happened: people wrote to him asking him to find them specific books, and other people offered him music books for sale. In short, he had found a niche in the market.

'I now deal mainly in music and poetry,' says John. 'I offer to find second-hand books for people. I know where to go and how to advertise for them because of my contacts in the book trade in the past. All my business is done through the phone and the post.'

Any enthusiasm – postcard, coin or stamp collecting for instance – could form the basis of a search service. Payment is usually strictly by results but if you know where to go to find things, you would quickly become known as a specialist and make a good income from the work.

Proof reading and indexing

If you have a meticulous eye, and an orderly mind, both these skills are relatively easy to learn, but to find the work you need contacts in the publishing industry. However, if you have some experience in this world, The Society of Indexers (see Help Section, page 193) would give you advice on courses to help you learn indexing, while the British Standard proof marks are listed in the *Writers' and Artists' Yearbook*.

Both indexers and proof readers are often paid by the job rather than by the hour. If you can read or index books on technical subjects you are likely to earn more. And to cut time, and save endless re-typing, a computer is vital for an indexing job.

With both proof reading and indexing you are likely to find yourself working against the clock, since the book is almost ready to go to press. Be prepared, as with manuscript typing, to work late and under pressure on occasions.

Hiring out

If you own, or can lay your hands on, the kind of things that people only want to use occasionally, you can make a useful income from hiring them out.

All sorts of things could be loaned out – garden machinery, DIY tools like electric saws and sanders, small-scale scaffolding, work benches. Then there are mountain bikes, even large-scale toys like scooters, tricycles, and dolls' houses.

Kathleen and John, who live in London, have built up a thriving business hiring out items like pushchairs, cots, and play pens, for people who visit the capital with their babies and want equipment for just a few days. 'We discovered that Mothercare were constantly being asked if they loaned out their things,' said John. 'They don't, of course, but now they recommend us if they get enquiries.'

They started off in a small way, picking up equipment from auction and car boot sales, setting up a repair workshop in their garage. 'Then we got hold of a free-sheet, a newspaper that consisted of nothing but advertisements, and had a circulation in an area where there were big estates of new houses,' said John. 'The people here all had young families, and we were surprised to find that they were so anxious to get rid of things like baby buggies and cots as the children grew up that they practically gave them away.'

A lick of paint here and there to their newly acquired equipment and they were in business. 'We painted everything in one distinctive colour and put the name of our hire company prominently on each item to discourage theft,' says John. They deliver and collect the items direct to their clients, visiting hotels and rented flats. 'We ask for the rental money up-front,' says John. 'If there is any problem, then we get a deposit.'

If you don't live in an area where short-term leasing of baby equipment would be appropriate, another variation would be to do long-term leasing instead, with the parents handing back items as the children out-grew them. However, this would involve more of your capital being tied up in stock.

Party hire

Jane, who found herself alone in a large, well-equipped house after her husband's death, discovered that she could hire out her dinner services, glassware and cutlery and large serving dishes – relics of a different life-style – to local hostesses for parties. 'I had to invest in containers to pack them in, but apart from that they are more than earning their keep,' she says. Initially she hired out her equipment to friends, but news of her reputation has spread, and the business is thriving. 'I have now actually started buying in equipment,' says Jane. 'I go to local auctions for things like unusual tureens and serving bowls, which I often pick up for next to nothing. I tend to buy classic dinner service patterns, however, so that the odd broken plate is easy to replace.' She has recently added table-linen to her list.

Dress hire

Special occasion dress hire is another avenue to explore. Couture garments can often be picked up for next to nothing from charity shops, and if you have a flair for fashion it might be worth a try. Marjorie runs a shop from her home that specialises in party clothes, many of them couture made. 'I get all sorts of people calling,' says Marjorie. 'And you get to hear their life histories. Many of them are wives who have to go to a special function with their husband, and don't want to waste money on buying something specially for it. My main expenses are dry cleaning – I have a bulk deal with a local shop – and doing running repairs.'

Occasional sports wear could be a very fruitful field. Riding gear, for instance, or ski wear. Other specialist areas worth considering are party clothes for children or complete wardrobes for pregnant mums.

Hats

Another possibility would be hats – nobody wants to spend a fortune on a hat for just one occasion. But if you already have quite a few, they might form the nucleus of a useful collection, to be borrowed for weddings, christenings and garden party use. If you are skilled with a needle, hat-making is a fascinating craft that is easily learned from books. (See also page 113.) For summer, you could offer something really special, like romantic straw hats trimmed with fresh flowers and delivered on the day of the event.

Hiring at home

If you already own some expensive fitness equipment like a jacuzzi, a heated swimming pool, a sun-bed, an exercise bike or a multi-gym, then consider having customers come to you to use it. It's vital to take out public liability insurance, of course, in case someone over-tans themself, gets a hernia lifting weights, or hits their head on the side of the pool.

Susan was left with a room full of fitness equipment after her husband ran off to live abroad with another woman. 'It had all belonged to Bob, but he didn't want to take it – it was too bulky. I planned to sell it off at first,' she says. 'Then a friend suggested I rented it out by the hour to people. Now I have a good business going and some new friends among the health freaks who come to use it. In fact, I'm planning to expand and buy more equipment.'

If you have people coming to your house to use sporting machines you will have to have a bathroom at their disposal, so they can shower afterwards. Don't forget to cost in the electricity the equipment uses, plus the cost of laundering towels.

Outworking

Doing work at home for an outside employer has a reputation for being poorly paid. It is generally rated as unskilled, and may well consist of putting something together, assembly line fashion, or doing some rather repetitive, boring job. However, if you find the right firm to work for, it can be a useful source of much-needed cash.

Beware of the cowboy firms, however. Don't enter into any kind of agreement where you are expected to spend money up-front to show that you are serious in your intentions. Don't take on anything which means you have to rent or even buy equipment from your employer, unless you are sure it is going to be worth while, and be careful that you don't find yourself working with unpleasant even dangerous things like adhesives that give off fumes. You may also find yourself being asked to store large quantities of materials, some of them flammable.

However, as a home worker, you are covered by the *Health and Safety at Work Act*, which should mean that your employer will not expose you to risks. And if you are working virtually full-time over a number of years, it is possible that you could qualify for redundancy if the firm dispensed with your services. (Consult your local Citizens' Advice Bureau.)

Outworkers are usually paid by the number of units or pieces they produce rather than by the hour. So, check, early on, just how many items you do produce in, and therefore earn by, the hour. Probably the best paid work is specialist machining, for which you need to be skilled in sewing – making buttonholes, putting on collars, finishing garments for the fashion trade. Here the production line method pays – avoid taking on fiddly things that need constant changes of cotton, for instance. Children's clothes are basically more tricky to do than those for grown-ups because of their small-scale size. Be careful, too, about hidden costs like needles, thread, even glues that you buy yourself for some types of job. Take them into account when deciding whether or not to go into this kind of work.

Laundry services

Many people loathe washing, ironing and mending, and would be happy to pay someone else to do these household chores if they could find such a paragon. A small-ad in your local paper should quickly bring in customers. If you are offering to wash the items, you don't necessarily have to have a huge washer-dryer, for you could use the local laundrette. Charge washing by the weight, and ironing by the item, checking out prices charged by local laundrettes and laundries. Invest in a cordless iron if you can, to make life easier for yourself, and things like a small sleeve board. You could offer a specialist shirt service for local businessmen – in that case invest in cellophane or clear plastic bags to pack the shirts in for a professional touch.

The days when socks and tights get darned may be almost over, but why not offer to do just that – and to replace trouser pockets, let out seams, other small chores.

Agencies

All you need is a telephone to set up an agency service of some kind, acting as a people-broker. Val, for instance, hit a bad patch when her husband's factory closed and he was made redundant. 'I knew that I had to go out and try and get some work,' she says. 'But I didn't have training in anything. I'd been a shop assistant before.' She decided to do the thing that she did well – house cleaning, and put an advertisement in the local paper offering her services.

'I was completely swamped with offers,' says Val. 'Then my husband said, 'If there are all those people out there wanting chars, why don't we find chars for them?' Val canvassed friends on her large housing estate, put cards in local shop windows, and in no time at all collected a team of women who liked the idea of earning extra pocket money. The result is a successful house-cleaning business – and Valerie earns money by taking commission from grateful home-owners.

Sheila, who juggled with a full-time job and two small children, relied on au pairs to keep the home going. 'Many of them became great friends,' she remembers. 'Brit, a Swedish girl came back to me two years running, and we actually went to Stockholm to stay with her family.' During that time Sheila met some of Brit's friends, who asked her if she could find families for them in England.

'It escalated from there,' says Sheila. 'I now run a busy au pair agency, specialising in girls from Denmark and Sweden. And Brit, who is now married with a baby of her own, handles the Scandinavian end for me.' Sheila reckons that her success is due to the in-depth questionnaires she has devised for both the host family and the au pairs.

There are a tremendous number of agency ideas out there for anyone who likes the idea of putting one set of people in touch with another. You have to be a 'people person', that is, able to talk to everyone and anyone, and make friends easily. Why not start a friendship agency for lonely people who want someone to go to the theatre or cinema with, even on holiday, for instance. Or you could even start up a marriage bureau.

There are all sorts of agencies that you could start from home, ranging from building repairs to a mini-cab service. It is best to stick to services that can be organised over the phone, rather than have people calling at your house. If you are running an agency connected with regular rather than casual employment, then you need a licence (see Help Section, page 193).

TURNING AN INTEREST INTO A BUSINESS

Pictures and antiques

While it would cost a fortune to open up an antique shop or picture gallery, if these are your consuming interests it is perfectly possible to deal from home, turning your house into a lived-in picture gallery or antique shop, with occasional forays to markets where you could take a stall. A house makes a perfect setting for antiques and bric-à-brac. Indeed, it is often much easier to sell pieces of furniture, or china if they are displayed in the kind of home setting where the buyer would want to put them. It is also a good place from which to deal in stamps, postcards, second-hand jewellery, all sorts of small items. Bill and Martha, a couple who live in a small country town, found that all the time they had, once they'd retired, hung heavily on their hands. They'd always been interested in bric-à-brac, and when Martha's mother died they took a stall in a local antiques market, held weekly in the village hall, where professional dealers had stands alongside amateurs. There they sold off some surplus china and brass from her home.

'We found that we really enjoyed selling,' says Martha. 'So much so, that we invested the money we took into more things, and started dealing that way.' They joined the antiques market circuit for a time, but then began to specialise in Staffordshire pottery and Victorian lustre ware, and Bill became skilled at repairing pieces of china, too. By now their hobby had become a consuming passion.

'After a while, we got tired of all the packing and unpacking of such fragile things, and the rushing around in the car,' said Martha. 'So we thought: Why not deal from home? And now we've done just that.' They found they were able to display their precious pieces in a more sympathetic setting, and ask higher prices for them. Dealers soon heard what they were doing and turned up on their doorstep. 'We were surprised to find that at least 75 per cent of the antiques trade consists of one dealer selling to another,' added Bill. They are so well known now that they don't need to advertise, but at first they put one or two discreet advertisements in the local paper, offering one specific item for sale and simply giving their phone number.

When it comes to dealing with the public from home, Bill and Martha have a rule: only one of them appears. 'We soon found that if you get two couples talking to one another it turns into a social occasion,' says Martha. 'You start talking about local restaurants, how bad the bus service is, things like that, and before you know it you've wasted an hour in chit-chat. One person serving makes it more business-like.'

A gallery

Charles had run a small picture gallery in London for years, specialising in small turn-of-the-century watercolours, when rising rents and rates and a dip in sales made him decide that it would have to close. 'It was economics really,' says Charles. 'My rent rose to almost £1,000 a week. I had always relied on visiting Americans for my trade, then suddenly the Americans weren't buying any more.'

He sold up and moved to an old rambling house in a village near Stratford-upon-Avon, and began dealing from home. 'I was surprised at how easy it was,' he says. 'The pictures looked much more attractive hung in a domestic setting, and I enjoy the more relaxed, sociable atmosphere you get, dealing this way. I can be more competitive on price, too, as I don't have so many overheads.'

Charles' wife, seeing a business opportunity in the constant stream of callers, some of whom needed somewhere to stay overnight, now does bed and breakfast for them. She also takes over the sales side when Charles is away buying more pictures.

'In fact, we are now unofficially on the tourist circuit,' says Charles. 'Foreigners in particular love to have the chance to stay in a real English home, it puts them in a mellow mood to buy.'

One lesson that Charles and his wife have learned is that they have to take their own personal pictures off the wall when visitors are expected. 'Otherwise, you can be sure that if they are told a painting is not for sale, that is the very one they want!'

If you are planning to deal from home, then you need an extrovert personality to be able to drum up business. 'It's difficult at first to ring someone and say I've got an amazing picture that is just right for you,' says Charles. 'But that's what you have to do to succeed. If you are dealing in something like fine art, you do really need to have had gallery experience of some sort, even if you only helped out at weekends. Otherwise people tend to lack faith in your judgement.'

If you are dealing in antiques or art from home you need a house that is large enough to display them without the buyer getting glimpses of shepherd's pie being made in the kitchen, or the washing machine roaring away. Even though the things are in a domestic setting, it's best to allocate one or two rooms only to the public. You will also need to ensure that either a grown-up handles the phone, or an answering machine is on – a childish voice piping 'hello' is fine if you are a craft worker, but sounds rather unnerving to a would-be buyer of paintings or antiques.

It goes without saying that if you have precious things in your house you must take out extra insurance and possibly install a safe. The premises should be made as burglar-proof as possible, and you should be discreet about what you are doing, so word does not get around among the criminal fraternity in the neighbourhood.

Creative writing

Over the years, many people who know I am an author have come up to me and said, 'I'm going to write a book, too, one day when I've got the time.' You may now be in just that situation. However, if you are hoping to make a good income out of your new chosen profession as an author, it has to be said that you have a tough time ahead. That doesn't mean you won't succeed, just that you will have to be persistent.

Fiction
Times are not good for novel writers. Publishers are cutting down drastically on the number of books that they print, and, in the case of fiction, are going more and more for big names. However, if you have a book in you that has to come out, then write it by all means, if you are prepared to regard it as a labour of love.

Having once written the novel you need to find an agent. Don't send it straight to a publisher for you will wait months before you get any response, and even then it may not have been read. They will, however, look at things that have been sent to them by a professional. And as far as agents are concerned you will have to be persistent even to find someone who is willing to read your work.

Don't be discouraged by all this, for if you have genuine talent, if what you have written is fresh, different and above all, compulsive reading, you may well make the grade – if you are resilient enough to stand being turned down, time and time again before you make the grade. Take heart: Frederick Forsyth's the *Day of the Jackal* was rejected out of hand by numerous publishers before he finally landed a contract. It *is* a risky business. Rosemary, a best-selling author with 32 published books to her credit says: 'Every time I produce the manuscript of a new book, I am laying myself on the line. You can't rely on past success any more to get published.'

Romantic fiction is a slightly different area. Mills and Boon, the publishers, actively encourage new talent and you don't have to send them your work via an agent. If this type of writing appeals to you, immerse yourself in their paper-backs until you feel you are in tune with what they want, note carefully the length of their books, send for their useful audio-tape for would-be authors (see Help Section, page 194), and start writing. To calculate the length of a book, by the way, take three lines at random on any page and word-count them (you might come up with: 10, 11 and 12), average the number of words to a line (11), multiply by the number of lines on the typed page (which might be 26), then by the number of pages of text in the book (say, 325). Always type your manuscript in double spacing, leaving a 1in margin at either side, and number each sheet. Always keep a copy yourself (in case the top copy is lost in the post) and enclose an appropriately sized, stamped addressed envelope for its possible return. Nowadays, many publishers prefer to receive a typed synopsis plus the first one or two chapters only. If their interest is captured, you will be asked to send in the remainder of the manuscript. If not, at least you will have saved on postage and wear and tear to the manuscript. New writers trying to interest an agent would benefit from adopting the same technique of submission. Enclose a *brief* covering letter and if you have had any previous publishing experience – say, several published short features in the local newspaper, don't forget to mention this. It shows enthusiasm and the likelihood that you are not just a one-off author, but would probably go on writing – with just a little positive encouragement!

Plays and film scripts

The BBC used to be very encouraging and helpful to new talent when it came to anything from the Morning Story on radio, to TV plays and sit-com series. The situation is bound to be different with the new changes taking place in the Corporation, but it is certainly worth trying them. If you are writing for an existing slot, such as *Play for Today*, note carefully the length of the broadcast piece: anything from half an hour to two hours and a half, and write accordingly. Calculate three words to a second when writing scripts both for radio and TV, set your scripts out as shown in text books on the subject.

If you have a really fresh and original idea, you may hit the jackpot and the BBC will work with you on it. Successful authors of many sit-coms would freely acknowledge the help that was given to them by the BBC in the early stages.

Writing is such a lonely business that keeping motivated can be difficult. That's why it pays to join a local Writer's Circle, even if you may not approve of their opinion of your work when you come to read it to them! Meeting other people who have the same interests and problems helps to keep you going. Subscribe to writing magazines too, and there are now many good writing courses to be had, notably those run by the Arvon Foundation (see Help Section, page 193).

Children

Writing for children has now become a very crowded market. Don't think because your family rave over your tales of Wuff the dog that complete strangers will take to it. As a publisher as well as a writer, I am constantly receiving very amateurish manuscripts of books for children which, the author assures me, are loved by their own family.

If you have something completely fresh to say to children – like a book of new nursery rhymes, or counting songs, then by all means try your hand. Who would have thought at the beginning that Roald Dahl's would have such best-selling appeal? If you have someone good to illustrate your stories, so much the better. Children's books are now very 'visual'. In fact, the tail is wagging the dog, and many children's artists write the text to go with their illustrations.

Freelance journalism

Many people have started their writing career this way. But as magazines and newspapers become more and more sophisticated in their requirements the standards they set make it difficult for a beginner to get in. Sending in an account of a neighbourhood flower show to the local paper is unlikely to get you far – they have probably sent their own reporter. If not, they expect to receive reports like that free of charge. The days when you could pen a self-indulgent article for the local press are over. In many ways, it is better to aim straight for the national papers, if you have a good story to tell.

At one time I earned money writing pieces like *They Fought Their Way to the Top* and *The Shame of Schoolgirl Mothers* for *The Sun* newspaper. The work was well paid, and I developed, temporarily, the thick skin needed to go with it. One of my difficult assignments was an interview with a nun ... The problem was she forgot she was being interviewed for a newspaper and was so frank about her feelings that I had a fantastic story. But I knew that if I published all that she actually said, it would put her in an untenable position. So I made the moral judgement to censor the story before submitting it. As newspapers go over more and more to features (television will always pip them to the post with hard news), there is space for well-written articles on emotive subjects like: Would you take him back, if you found he was having an affair? provided you could lace them with interviews with actual people who have been through this kind of problem. Plunder your friends, but change their names and the places where they live, of course – and get their permission. Many women magazines, too, are hungry for material like this, if you are able to turn out a slick piece. If you are writing for newspapers on a regular basis you may need to join the National Union of Journalists (see Help Section, 193).

The market

Study the market, don't waste your time and money sending pieces to the wrong people. In the years when I was a magazine editor I had a constant flood of articles sent to me on subjects that bore no relation to those we published. Note the average length of features, and check whether the magazine will look at your work. Some publications – *Cosmopolitan*, for instance – have a notice on their contents page saying that they do not look at unsolicited work.

Journalists are busy people, haunted by deadlines, and no editor is going to be bothered to hack your copy back if it is too long, or ask you to send them another two hundred words, however well it is written. And don't try to sell coals to Newcastle – fashion magazines will not want an article on the latest fashions, though they may take an in-depth interview with a new young designer. Gardening magazines will not take general gardening pieces; they have their own staff writers and regular contributors for that. However, if you have a very specialist knowledge on, say hellebores, or gardens of America and can provide good transparencies, properly captioned, then you may be in.

Travel writing

Travel writing sounds very seductive – you choose where you want to go, get a free airline ticket, then get paid for writing about it. At one time this theory might have been true, and indeed, travel writing took me twice around the world. However, I was attached to a magazine at the time (almost all publications have their own travel editor) and economic forces have changed all that. Airlines are very unlikely to give free tickets to would-be writers, even if you do get a letter from a magazine commissioning you to do a piece, and hotels are not keen to give you a room. However, if you are going somewhere really unusual, if you are attending a festival that no one has ever heard about – like, say, a wedding feast in the Sahara – then try publications that feature travel heavily, in the hope that they will look at your report when you get back.

Photography

If you are a skilled amateur photographer and specialise in something like child or animal portraiture, it is still possible to earn money this way, since the large firms that specialise in things like weddings are not likely to extend their energies in other directions. Photographs of people's houses and gardens are another area worth exploring. Another possibility is offering a service photographing jewellery and other valuables for insurance purposes.

You could also specialise in another way – taking photographs of artists' work, for instance, or that of tapestry makers and embroiderers. You could take the service even further, and have your pictures made up into postcards for them. There are many specialist firms now who would do the printing for you.

If you happen to live in an area of natural beauty or tourist interest, and can take interesting and unusual pictures, then consider doing photographs for your own range of postcards and selling them in the local shops. You could also try your hand at covering local events like gymkhanas, flower shows, sporting occasions, and big parties. You could, for instance, approach the proud prizewinner at a local show, and offer a portrait of them with their trophy. A useful spin-off would be to offer pictures to local papers and county magazines.

It is difficult to break into the wedding market as it has been efficiently sewn up by firms which produce albums of pictures before the wedding breakfast has finished. However, it might well be worth-while scrutinising the local paper for lists of engagements, christenings, and silver weddings and offer your services. Be prepared to show some examples of work you have already done.

Studio
To succeed as a photographer you will probably need a well lit studio, which will involve buying lighting equipment, having an efficient darkroom and a good colour processor laboratory to call on (the best ones will do film for you in under two hours). Get your supplies of film, printing paper and chemicals from a wholesaler. Having invested money in studio facilities and a darkroom, consider letting them out to enthusiastic amateurs as a profitable sideline.

Cameras
You will almost certainly find that after a while you will need more than one camera, and you may also decide, as many professional photographers do, that a polaroid camera is useful so you can show customers instantly the sort of picture that they are going to get. Present your photographs attractively – photographic magazines are full of advertisements offering cards and mounts – and be sure to buy your film wholesale to save money.

A picture library
If you have assembled a large collection of colour transparencies over the years on any particular subject, setting up your own picture library is another photographic possibility. Publishers of both books and magazines are always looking for unusual pictures in specialised subjects – perhaps of one particular country, or of gardens, wildflowers, or animals, and will pay high prices to use them. Make up a catalogue of what you can offer, then write to likely prospects in the publishing world (glean them from a copy of the *Writers' And Artists' Yearbook*). You will need to get your transparencies duplicated so that you always keep the master. And despatch them in protective, transparent sleeves to avoid possible damage from excessive fingering. Sandwich them between protective card – and register the package. You should take out insurance against loss. To find out what reasonable fees you should charge, contact one or two picture agencies as a potential customer (look in *Writers' And Artists' Yearbook*).

OTHER INTERESTS THAT COULD BE PROFITABLE

If **Astrology** is your passion, there are plenty of how-to books to be had on this fascinating subject, if you have an aptitude for it and a genuine interest. The only equipment you need are the ephemerides, astrological almanacs which tell you where the planets are at certain times of the day over the years, and blank charts for you to fill in the customer's stellar details (buy them from specialist shops – look in astrology magazines). You could then do people's charts by post or they could come for a personal visit. **Graphology, Tarot, I Ching** and reading the **Runes** are other subjects that can be studied and certainly bring in customers. Many people are also interested in **Bio-rhythms**. Reference books, complete with charts to work with, are also on sale in specialist 'magic' shops and some booksellers.

Advertise all these services first of all in your local paper. Then go on to taking small advertisements in specialist magazines. However if you are good, your fame will spread quickly by word of mouth.

Using Your Skills: Arts and Crafts

Basketry and canework ... Découpage ... Papier mâché ... Weaving ... Patchwork and appliqué ... Batik ... Silk screen printing ... Tie and dye ... Painting on silk ... Dressmaking ... Hatmaking ... Quilting ... Soft furnishings ... Knitting ... Embroidery and needlepoint ... Soft toys ... Pottery ... Jewellery making ... Jewellery repairs ... Model-making ... Toy making ... Toys and accessories for animals ... Furniture restoration ... Upholstery ... Repairing china and glass ... Bookbinding ... Picture framing ... Painting ... Illustration work ... Art restoration ... Glass decoration ... Calligraphy ... Candle-making ... Painted furniture ... Artificial flowers ... Paper making ...

WORKING ON A CRAFT FROM YOUR HOME, whether it's needlework, candlemaking, or furniture decoration, for instance, poses no planning problems. You are free to do as you like, provided the activity of your choice does not annoy the neighbours – a welding shop, for instance could be noisy.

What you *will* find, however, is a lot of competition, for almost everyone with a creative bent dreams of making beautiful objects and selling them – and it is the sales side that counts.

If it is money you're after, you may have to be prepared to put your own good taste on the back burner. You could, for instance, make the most amazing garden sculptures, but find that what the public wants, in quantity, are painted concrete gnomes. But if you are prepared to wait for eventual acceptance rather than sacrifice your principles, then soldier on with your chosen designs.

Or it could be that just a small change is needed to make your product sell. A particular case in point is a friend of mine, Marie, an impassioned weaver, who makes wonderful pieces of cloth in stained glass colours. Unfortunately, having woven them, she doesn't know what to do with them, and turns them into shapeless, bad-fitting sweaters that nobody wants to buy. If she switched to making rugs, pram covers or bed-spreads she would probably find a ready market for them.

Many techniques can be learned. Remember, it's the extra plus factor – your individual talent and ideas – that makes your product different from all the rest, and therefore desirable.

DECORATIVE CRAFTS

Basketry and cane work

The Far East has got this particular craft well covered and is flooding the market with cheap baskets and basketwork chairs that would undercut anything you could provide. So, if this is your interest, you need to make a better basket using traditional rushes, willow or reeds and look, particularly in continental magazines, for unusual shapes and ideas. At the time of writing, little baskets made from twigs and filled with dried flowers are all the rage in France, and command high prices.

Re-caning chairs is a skill that is well worth learning, for the old days when tradesmen used to call at the door offering to re-cane your chairs have long since gone, and many people are at a loss to know where they can get the work done. That is where you step in. Caning is not nearly as difficult to do as it appears. In fact it is a craft that can be learned quite easily from books or at craft classes. Having mastered the skill you could look out for chairs in need of repair at knock-down prices, re-cane them and re-sell them. Suitable cane can be bought at most good craft shops or by post through advertisements in craft magazines. If you find yourself doing a lot of this work, then you would need to track down wholesale supplies.

Découpage

The Victorian skill of découpage is very much in fashion at the moment and very easy to learn. Basically, it consists of cutting out pictures from magazines, or buying sheets of what are called 'scraps' and glueing them on to objects made of wood, glass or metal – in fact, any surface they can be glued to. There are many courses to be had on the subject but it is extremely easy to learn. The art in découpage lies in what you do with the surface of the paper. By gently sanding down rough stuck-down edges of the paper, and by applying dozens of coats of clear varnish – sometimes antiqueing them by applying a crackle finish, then a dark shade of shellac – you can create exquisite looking cigarette boxes, jewellery cases, and all manner of small objects. Or you can be bold and cover a whole screen or even a table top.

Craft shops and craft magazines are the sources from which to buy your basic shapes, and mail-order firms dealing in paper (see Help Section, page 194), can sell you sheets of Victorian or modern 'scraps' as they are called. These cover all manner of subjects, from cut-out flowers, animals, birds, to children, fashions, cars and cottages. Meanwhile, making a practice of going through all your magazines and tearing out anything that might come in handy, and next time you're in London, visit the Victoria and Albert Museum to see examples of découpage at its best.

Sell your pieces into local decoration shops and at craft fairs. If you build up a large collection and become well known, then people will come and visit you.

Papier mâché

Papier mâché has a great deal going for it as a craft. The materials are virtually free – you'll be using discarded newspapers – and most items that you might need for moulds can be found around the house. It's easy to learn to do, and it is completely versatile. We think of it mainly in terms of bowls and other small decorative objects, but at one time it was even used for making furniture.

There are two ways of working with papier mâché: you can either build up layers of pasted paper over a mould, or you can mash the soaked paper with glue and sculpt it. Either way, there is no end to the things you can make from it. Plates, bowls, boxes, picture and mirror frames are just a few of the items you'll find made from papier mâché in the shops. But you can also sculpt it into inventive lightweight jewellery, especially earrings and bracelets, setting stones in it, or gilding it for extra effect. And you can make superb toys like jointed Victorian-style dolls. Or you can build it over an iron armature to make larger pieces.

You can make it extra strong by adding acrylic varnish or glue in with the water in which the paper is soaked. You can speed up the drying process by putting pieces in a microwave, and you can even waterproof your papier mâché by brushing it over with linseed oil then baking it in a low oven. Once dry, the pieces can be painted as if they were made of wood.

To see some of the best examples of papier mâché work, visit the Victoria and Albert Museum, and shops that have handmade craft items on sale – Liberty's, for instance. Sell your own work through local boutiques and at craft fairs.

TEXTILE CRAFTS
Weaving

This is another area where there seem to be more people producing woven items than there are buyers for their product. But this fact need not put off the really committed weaver. However, if you are intending to sell your work, you may need to switch to a larger, more versatile loom than the one you have at present; for many table-top looms can only produce fabric of a narrow width.

A beautiful piece of hand-made cloth can be made into a number of things – a throw, for instance, which can be used variously as a travel rug, a shawl, or displayed over a chair or sofa. Pieces of cloth can be made up into simple tabard type tops, or ponchos. They also make good covers for prams, cots and childrens' beds. If particularly decorative, they make excellent wall hangings.

Woven rag rugs

Gwen decided to turn her passion for weaving into a way of earning money, but had to spend cash at first buying a larger second-hand loom which gave her more scope. She switched from doing fine woven things like scarves and squares to rugs and almost immediately found a market for them. 'I chose bright Mexican-style colours, primary reds, blues and yellows, and found that people liked to buy them for places like a child's playroom or a breakfast room,' says Gwen. 'Then I began to offer a specialised service, making up rag rugs in colours that complemented my clients' kitchens, and other work rooms in the house. I also wove a rag rug for one woman using off-cuts of the furnishing fabric and curtain materials in her country living room. The result, set on a polished pine floor, was so good that it appeared in a decoration magazine.'

Markets

Spotting a marketing opportunity like this will make all the difference from the sales point of view in this very crowded craft. If you know, and could work in tandem with a successful dressmaker, you could offer colour co-ordinated scarves, stoles and sweaters to her customers to go with the clothes that she makes them, for a really unique look. In the same way, you could offer your services to a local interior decorator, making rugs and cushions that are completely individual and exclusive. Get yourself known by not only showing your goods at craft markets but taking them to local boutiques and decoration shops – they are always looking for something different to offer their customers. If you are already a weaver, you don't need me to tell you that you need a room dedicated to your craft. Weaving is not just a hobby, more a way of life!

Patchwork and appliqué

There's been an enormous up-surge of interest in these particular textile crafts over recent years, and more and more people are aiming to make a living from them. Basically this skill is now divided up into two groups: the traditional and the modern, for there's a break-away group of patchworkers who are seeking to find new ways of using scraps of fabric, not just for bed coverings but combining it with appliqué and quiltings for decorative wall panels and hangings on a par with pictures.

Traditional

Traditional patchwork – basic diamonds and hexagonals – makes pretty country style quilts that are much sought after. However, over recent years entrepreneurs in the textile business have had quilts of this kind made for them by low-waged workers in India and the Far East. And though you may find a market for the traditional quilts that you have slaved over, you may also find it difficult to get a price for them that reflects all the time you put in.

There are ways round this, of course. If you go for the more unusual designs – log cabin for instance, or tumbling blocks, that are not easily done by mass production methods then you are more likely to get a realistic price for your efforts. You could also specialise in personalised quilts to order: one covered with appliquéd flowers and animals for a new baby for instance, an ABC bedcover for a toddler, or a romantic heritage quilt for a bride, adding your own particular touch of talent to the design.

Patchwork is an easy craft to learn from books. You can pick up interesting how-to books and leaflets from America at craft fairs. Many shops now sell what are known as 'craft fabrics' from the USA, textiles with small all-over patterns that are particularly good for quilts. Craft shops and the haberdashery department in big stores will sell the templates you need for your shapes. The tools you use are few – you don't even have to have a sewing machine since the best quilts are always done by hand. But you will need to build up a fabric 'library' to pick your pieces from. Haunt sales for remnants, root through second-hand clothes at jumble and car boot sales – an ideal source of faded fabrics that will give your work an antique look. Store your fabrics in colour groups on racks, so you can see at a glance what you have to work with. Try mixing appliqué with patchwork, cutting out motifs and glueing then stitching them in place.

... and modern

If, on the other hand, you are making decorative modern wall hangings in patchwork and appliqué, rather than bedspreads and cushions, you are basically in the same league as the professional painter. You are producing a piece of work that stands on its own as an artistic object. And whether the public buy or not depends on their taste, and yours. Try to get an exhibition of your work shown in a local gallery, give framed pieces to local decoration shops on a sale or return basis, exhibit at craft fairs, and see what happens.

PRINTING AND DYEING
Batik

Although many people are making a living from this fascinating craft of working on a base fabric with hot wax and colourful dyes, this technique gives you endless opportunities to produce really original pieces – from silk scarves in wonderful colours to pictures and wall hangings. Remember, if you are planning a production line, to keep a card for each piece, noting meticulously the dyes that you used, where the basic fabric came from and what colour it was. Batik pieces can be sold in craft shops, direct to the public at fairs or, in the case of scarves, to fashion boutiques. Most book shops or libraries with a craft section will be able to recommend one or two good books on the subject if it is new to you and you would like to know more.

Silk screen printing

Silk screening is basically a form of stencilling, when the ink or dye is forced through a fine screen, usually made from nylon mesh. It is an easy skill to learn via evening classes, probably at the local art school. And if you enjoy working with silk screens you can turn out anything from patterns on tee-shirts to fine silk squares via table cloths and cushions. If you are more ambitious still, you could even print fabric by the yard. You can also screen on to paper, producing greetings cards, limited edition prints, or paper blinds.

The saleability of what you make depends on your own artistic flair for colour and shapes. One thing is certain: you need a separate workshop in which to pursue this rather messy craft, with somewhere to store screens, dyes and glues. As with other crafts of this kind, your best bet is to sell through local boutiques, through craft fairs and, eventually to personal customers through the post.

Tie and dye

In its hey-day in the late 1960s and early 1970s, tie and dye now shows signs of making a fashion come-back. Like batik, it is a resist dying process – you knot, fold or sew parts of a piece of cloth in such a way that when it is dipped in a dye bath the colour cannot reach those parts. You can do this not just once but several times, so that the colours overlap, making very sophisticated designs. String and stones, buttons, all sorts of objects are used to vary the pattern.

If this way of working with textiles appeals to you, you can either use the craft to produce decorative wall hangings and cushion covers or take simple garments like tee shirts and plain cotton jersey tunics, skirts and dresses, and turn them into works of art that might well sell in local boutiques, especially as holiday wear. You could try also making to order curtains using tie and dye patterns – do a sample length to show prospective customers what you can do. Tie and dye is very easily learned with the aid of textbooks on the subject – you should be able to find them in your public library.

Painting on silk

Fabric paints and dyes have become so sophisticated now that painting on silk has become an art rather than just a craft. You can either use raw silk in its unbleached state or dye to a colour of your choice, then stretch it on a frame and paint on it. If you have real artistic talent, coupled with a love of working with textiles, painted silk scarves might well bring you in a good reward. There are plenty of courses and classes to be found in this subject, and books, too.

USING YOUR NEEDLE

If you're keen on sewing, the opportunities to use your talents are endless, its just a case of picking which particular market is right for you:

Dressmaking

As a small child, I dreaded regular visits to the dressmaker, when I was expected to stand still for what seemed hours, while she circled round me with a mouth full of pins. But things have changed, few people have their clothes specially made for them by individuals, unless they are rich enough to go to a couturier. The kind of people who patronise a dressmaker these days are those that don't for some reason or other fit into the criteria of British Standard sizing. They'll be extra short, or tall, or more probably, somewhat large in the beam and unable to find attractive clothes to fit them.

Cutting patterns
They will be grateful to hear of your service, of course, but that doesn't mean that they will accept anything other than a

top-class finish – couture rather than ready-to-wear. This could be your line, if you are good at making clothes with a really top-class finish. Pattern-cutting is a skill that any intelligent dressmaker should acquire if she does not already know how to do it. There are plenty of books to be had on the subject. Try R.D. Franks of London (see Help Section page 194) if you cannot lay your hands on one locally – though your public library should be able to help. I learned to cut and grade patterns with the aid of a simple how-to book, and was soon proficient enough to do them for my own children's wear manufacturing business.

Equipment you need

I assume that you already have a good steam iron, and an up-to-date, reliable electric sewing-machine. It needs to have a swing needle so that you can zig-zag over raw edges. Indeed, if you are going in for dressmaking in a really professional way, it would certainly pay you to buy an overlocker. Caroline, a keen home sewer who found herself suddenly made redundant from her office job, decided to spend some of her pay-off money on an overlocker since she was planning to make dressmaking her new career. She finds it has more than paid for itself already in time-saving alone. She didn't buy a new one, but found a second-hand machine on sale quite reasonably in a shop specialising in equipment for the garment trade.

Most customers, Caroline finds, come with only a hazy idea of what they want. So she has begged from her local fabric shop old pattern catalogues they can thumb through, and, incidentally, put a card up on their notice board advertising her services. One of the most difficult tasks a dressmaker may face is gently persuading the customer that she is the wrong shape and age for, say, a snappy little number photographed on Madonna. If the fabric is draped on an adjustable dressmaker's dummy, let out to their size, this will sometimes hammer the message home.

Costing

Like most dressmakers, Caroline charges by the hour, costing in trimmings she may have to hunt down in the shops. Occasionally she will give an estimate for a dress if it looks like being a particularly elaborate one, but she prefers to work on a time basis. She does fittings in her bedroom, which is warm and has a full-length mirror, and she tries to see customers in the day only, when her family are out to avoid the embarrassment of her husband going into the bedroom inadvertently and catching someone in their petticoat.

Weddings

'Wedding dresses are the most difficult ones to do,' says Caroline. 'The bride's mother tends to interfere, and more often than not she and the bride-to-be often arrive with expensive fabric which is quite unsuitable for the style that has been chosen, and have to be gently talked out of the idea. It's hard work, but I often get invited to the wedding and it does give me a thrill to see my dress going up the aisle.' However, there is no doubt that this is one of the most lucrative kinds of dressmaking, especially if you land an order for the bridesmaids' dresses too.

There are all sorts of ways in which you could specialise on the dressmaking front. You could be known for your children's party clothes, for instance, or for making inventive fancy dress outfits. Or you could be particularly skilled and sympathetic at making clothes for the elderly or very overweight people who are embarrassed to undress and try on clothes in a store. Much of your success, apart from your sewing skills, will stem from your relationship with your customers. They need to trust you, and you, in your turn, have to like people.

Running repairs

At the other end of the scale, doing alterations to shop-bought clothes can bring in plenty of cash. You have to be very confident of what you are doing, however, before you start hacking away at a hem or shortening a sleeve. Few shops now offer an alteration service, or if they do it is expensive and slow. If this kind of work appeals to you, it might pay you to contact local boutiques and ask them to pass customers on to you. Repairs such as putting in new zips or trouser pockets or renewing linings are another source of work, albeit a rather dreary one, for the home dressmaker. The best place to advertise your skills here is at the local dry-cleaners. If they don't have someone behind the scenes doing this work, they might well to glad to hear of you and pass you jobs.

Hat making

Making hats is a relatively easy skill to learn once you have mastered the techniques of blocking and steaming felt hoods. It is also something that you can learn at one of the many courses and evening classes held on the subject. Once you have the basic knowledge under your belt, you can then turn out big beautiful hats for special occasions, either selling them direct to the public or via local boutiques.

Susanna makes her hats in a converted outbuilding attached to her cottage in Oxfordshire and sends them all over the world. She works mainly in straws, organzas and silks because she finds, 'In Britain, we are much more inclined to splash out on a best straw hat for a garden party or spring wedding.' She made her first hat when she was six years old, and has never doubted what she wanted to do. Now she has a team of outworkers who do the hand-stitching and finishing while she designs hats that are sold from New York to Sydney. She prefers working from home: 'For my work, I could easily live in London, but I don't want to live in a rarefied fashion environment.' She uses straws and felts, which are easily obtained from specialist suppliers.

Quilting

Quilted objects have suddenly become very fashionable, whether it is white on white stitchery in traditional Welsh designs, quilted petticoats, Provençal fashion, or big beautiful covers for a bed.

If you are able to do hand quilting there is a market out there for exquisite cushions and bedcovers, but it is very demanding work. Otherwise, consider offering customers quilted cushions to match their loose covers or curtains – done simply by backing the fabric with batting then running the sewing machine around the shape of the flowers or other large motifs in the material. Offer a service, too, making duvet covers in the same way, to give a bedroom a co-ordinated look.

Trapunto
This is an ancient form of quilting where cord or cotton wool is stuffed between lines of stitching to give a raised effect. This luxurious looking stitchery can be used for all kinds of things, from three dimensional patterns on silk jackets or the hem of a skirt to tracing out the features on the face of a doll. Learn the techniques of trapunto from good embroidery books.

Soft furnishings

You only have to wander through the busy furnishing fabric section of any large store – branches of John Lewis for instance – to see that at any given time a large number of people in this country are changing their curtains – a lucrative potential source of income for anyone who is good at making soft furnishings.

If you're a keen home sewer, it's easy to learn to make curtains and loose covers to a high professional standard with the aid of books. The intricacies of pleated headings, scalloped tops and pelmets are surprisingly easy to master; so are the calculations needed. There are evening classes, too, in this particular branch of sewing throughout the country.

Offering a service
Offering a soft furnishing making service as a freelance, you have one big advantage over the service offered by local shops. You give the customer the freedom to buy her materials wherever she likes (most shops will only make up fabric that the customer has bought direct from them). And you will almost certainly be speedier.

Work space

You'll need a good working space – ideally a sewing room where you can leave everything out, certainly a large table and a good sewing machine with attachments like a special foot for piping, plus a first class iron. Insist on doing your own measuring up and, in the case of loose covers, fitting them on to the furniture at tacking stage. Never trust someone else's calculations.

If your business prospers, you might make extra money by buying some of the fabric wholesale for your customers – curtain linings for instance – and putting on your own mark-up (or profit) and selling it to them at just under the ordinary retail price. To do this, however, you would have to shift large quantities of fabric since wholesalers will not deal in small amounts. The same goes for trimmings like tassels and decorative rope tie-backs.

Blinds

Blinds are very much in vogue at the moment, especially the ruched varieties like Roman and Austrian shades. The mechanism for them is easily bought, and making the blinds is an area you might like to consider specialising in. Most shop-bought blinds come in standard sizes only, and uninspiring colours – this is where you could score. You could also paint on the blinds or appliqué shapes with glue – a row of tulips along the bottom for instance, or seagulls wheeling overhead.

Cushions and lampshade covers are another off-shoot of soft furnishings that can be very profitable to make if you do something special. Or you could make things like fun cushions in towelling for the bathroom, and special ones for a nursery.

You could then follow up by making matching lampshades by a mixture of stitching and glueing. Wire frames for shades can now be bought almost everywhere. Once again, this is a skill that can be learned easily from a book. Be aware of how fashions in lampshades are going – look in magazines like *Homes and Gardens*, and *Country Living*, to see what other people have in their homes. Check out the lampshades in your local store, also. Later, you might like to have a go at making lampshades to sell in local boutiques to boost your earnings.

Knitting

Really inventive knitted jackets and sweaters reach phenomenal prices in the shops now. And there are now many small designers all over the country turning out knitted clothes, some of them from hand-dyed yarns, so the competition is stiff. If you are able to make up your own artistic and colourful patterns and designs, then start in a small way, selling through local fashion boutiques, progress to exclusive shops and stores like Liberty in London, and as demand grows consider going into the mail order market.

Knitters are always needed as outworkers, but this can be a form of slave labour – it depends how fast you can work. Before a company takes you on they will want to see some of your finished work, and a small knitted sample to make sure that you can knit to the correct tension.

Machines

Machine knitting is a totally different craft, one that many hand-knitters fail to come to terms with. It is, however, much quicker, and the yarn that you work with is cheaper. Before rushing out to buy a machine, it's vital to get as much information about it as you can. Many adult education colleges run courses in machine knitting now, and you should look at several different models of machine before making up your mind. If you are not automatically offered a full demonstration of the model's capabilities and a chance to try it yourself, then ask.

If you are working with a machine instead of just a pair of needles, you will need a separate workroom, ideally, in which to set it up.

If you are selling direct, cost in your time realistically. Even if you enjoy knitting, you should be paid well for it! Package the finished products as attractively as possible, so that they look like luxury garments. Have your own labels woven to sew in at the neck, and use cellophane rather than ordinary plastic bags to display them in.

Embroidery and needlepoint

Both these skills are now extremely fashionable. Here again, however, cheap labour from third world countries is being used to produce cushions and pictures, now on sale in the shops at prices that it is impossible to compete with. So this is where you use your ingenuity, as these people have done.

Annie has always been keen on needlepoint and now makes a good living stitching cushions and pictures adorned with portraits of people's pets. She combines her sewing skills, of course, with the ability to paint on the canvas – blowing up photographs and then transferring them. She is thinking of going on to embroider pictures of customers' houses and gardens as another way of making money.

Edith does exquisite embroidery on hand towels, sheets and pillowcases for a ritzy bed-linen boutique. She also embroiders handkerchiefs, which sell well at Christmas time. Now she has just had her first order from America and has taken on an apprentice.

If you are really gifted in embroidery or needlepoint design, consider selling your services to the firms who supply kits. They would want to see samples both of your drawing on the linen or canvas, and the finished work. Or you could start to supply your own individual kits direct to the public. Elizabeth Bradley, whose needlepoint kits sell all over the world, started in a small way from home.

Soft toys

Soft toys, whether they are knitted or sewn, have a particular appeal, especially at Christmas time. If they have a second use, as a nightdress case or a shoe-bag for instance, then you have a double chance of selling them.

Remember that, as with children's books, they need to appeal to the adult who is giving them as presents as much as to the child who receives them, if they are to sell well. Use your imagination to conjure up new creatures, but avoid anything that is an existing film or TV character – Paddington Bear, Micky Mouse and other characters of worldwide renown are all covered by strict copyright regulations and you could be in trouble if you made your own for sale.

The scope is enormous, from dolls and teddies down to cuddly farm animals and even space-age figures, or dinosaurs. Bear in mind that they are going to have to stand up to a great deal of wear and tear. The material from which they are made must not be flammable – and that includes the stuffing, of course. It is best if they are washable, and they should not have dangerous things like eyes on wires, or indeed anything attached to them that a child might just swallow. To check that the things you are planning to make are considered safe, you need to get a copy of the regulations covering toys (see Help Section, page 194).

The best way to succeed in a soft toy business is to specialise, so that you become known for your Victorian dolls or your teddies. Dolls' clothes, which are often so badly made, could be another useful outlet for your talents if you have the patience to make miniature garments. Take your measurements from popular selling dolls like Cindy and Barbie for instance, look out for 'craft' fabrics on sale for patchwork in the sewing department of stores. They have small all-over patterns that suit small dolls well. Look out also for remnants at sales time, and patchwork pieces – then save them. You could offer a service creating a complete wardrobe for individual dolls – ideal for Christmas presents.

USING YOUR HANDS

If you are handy with a hammer, if you can work with metals, repair furniture, make jewellery, or perhaps pottery, then you have a talent at your finger-tips that might well turn into a lucrative career. Or you may have some other consuming interest that you have been pursuing for years, and never thought of capitalising on. Book binders and glass engravers, for instance, can command high prices for their work, and once you are known you will receive commissions.

Pottery

If you can make good quality pottery that is both interesting and imaginative, then you could and should be able to find a market for it. You might, for instance, consider making dolls' tea sets, ceramic jewellery, small things at first, and find a more ready sale for them than from conventional vases and jugs.

If you're starting from scratch, do take a course first before being tempted to invest in items like a kiln, and especially a wheel – many successful potters do not use one at all.

This is a home-based job that needs proper premises. Maybe the garage can be converted, or an outside shed. But you'll need electricity laid on to run a kiln. Electric ones are the only sensible choice, certainly if you are a beginner. You will also need a sink, of course, plenty of space to store things like half-finished pots, and sacks of clay. You will also be working with chemicals in the form of glazes, so you need to be able to work well away from the reach of children, and it's sensible to use an industrial mask and protective gloves when you are handling them.

Join the Craftsmen Potters' Association (see Help Section, page 194). If your work is of a high enough standard they will make you a member. Failing that, become an associate member for the time being. Their shop in London gives regular exhibitions of work, and yours might be included in one.

Avoid falling into the trap where you are making things on a repetitive basis. An order for, say, a hundred identical mugs might sound financially appealing but would pall, after a while! And remember when you are doing your costings that you need to allow for the inevitability of some things cracking at firing stage, glazes going wrong.

Heather became a potter, as she says, 'Almost by accident. My third child was off to nursery school and suddenly I had some time. I wandered along to the local institute with a friend who said she'd always wanted to try pottery – and I was hooked!' Heather found herself spending more and more time at her wheel. 'I made a coffee set and put it in a local exhibition. It went straight away, and I got orders for four more. I had to learn to throw quickly after that!' She is now an established full-time potter, and teaches part-time, at the institute where she first tried working with clay.

Jewellery making

The amount of skill you need for jewellery-making depends entirely on the type of piece you are going to make. At its most basic, you could easily teach yourself to string colourful beads into necklaces, bracelets or even ear-rings and brooches. At the other end of the scale you could be trained to work with silver, gold and precious stones.

The more expensive the material you are working with, the more equipment you will need. A halfway house between the simple and the skilled type of jewellery making would be to construct brooches, rings and necklaces using unusual pebbles and semi-precious stones. You might live near the sea, for instance, and be able to pick up interesting shells and pebbles on the beach. For this craft you could buy a noisy but effective tumbling machine second-hand, cheaply, through craft magazines. You would also need a soldering iron (which must *never* be used on precious metals like silver or gold) and some glues. Teach yourself to do the setting with the aid of books. It is easy to buy items like necklace fastenings, ear clips and brooch pins from craft shops.

Jewellery repairs

There is always a demand for a repair service for jewellery, and if this particular aspect of jewellery making appeals to you, then consider the possibility of learning how to do it. Bear in mind that it actually takes more skill to repair a broken piece of jewellery than it does to start from scratch. However, provided you keep well away from precious metals and stones, many people would be glad to have someone who would re-string beads for them, or repair favourite ear-rings or a brooch that has a fake jewel missing from it.

Start by practising on broken necklaces and other items of costume jewellery borrowed from friends or picked up at car boot sales. If you find you have the necessary flair for it you could then go on to buy broken pieces, restore them, and re-sell them.

Model making

If you are already involved in this very precise hobby, there could be many outlets for your work. Local architects and surveyors, also large firms that habitually exhibit at trade fairs could all be interested in your services. And when the housing market picks up, builders starting on a new estate might well want model houses to show would-be customers. Build up a portfolio of photographs of your work and contact them.

You could also make model landscapes to go with train or farm sets and sell them through local toy-shops. Another specialised service you could offer through the post or by advertising in the local paper would be to proud home-owners, offering them a model version of their house to sit on the mantelpiece.

Toy making

There's a whole spectrum of toys to be made by anyone who has carpentry skills, from old-fashioned rocking horses to dolls' houses. These, too, are governed by certain regulations (see Help Section, page 194), most of them based on common sense. For example, a special animal seat made for a child must be strong enough to bear its weight (and probably that of an adult who will try to sit in it!). You must also be careful about sharp edges, and moving parts that might be swallowed. And never use paint containing lead.

The fascinating world of dolls' houses opens up to anyone who wants to work from home, provided they have a work-space in which to make them. You could make a model of the child's actual home in miniature, for instance. Even if your carpentry skills are minimal, there is a lot of scope in making dolls' furniture, using card, balsawood and all sorts of materials to create three-piece suites, four-poster beds, tables and chairs.

Jenny has cornered a very specialised section of the market. She makes plates of food for dolls' houses and to go with dolls' tea-sets too, fashioning pies, cakes, and puddings – in fact, anything from a hamburger to a roast beef dinner on a plate. 'I use self-hardening modelling clay,' she says, 'which I varnish and paint. I sell a great deal by post, and that's simple, because they are so easy to pack.'

Toys and accessories for animals

Making things for pets is a specialist craft business that could bring you in a good income, needing as it does a mixture of sewing and carpentry skills, depending on what you are planning to produce.

Cats are a good market to cater for. You could make toys for them, for instance, such as fabric mice stuffed with dried cat-mint, and attractive jewel-studded collars based on elastic.

If you are clever at working with leather, there is a whole market out there for interesting and unusual collars for both cats and dogs – perhaps with their names featured on them in studs. Attractive, stylish overcoats for dogs in different shapes and sizes would also find a market, particularly if they have some kind of immediate appeal.

Joan specialises in unusual animal collars. Currently she is doing well with poodle collars in tartan taffeta ribbon, crowned with a large bow. Last winter, she made bow-tie collars in black and white, and they went well, as did sparkling collars at Christmas time. Long ago, when 'Dallas' was big on the television screens, Joan made a series of dog coats with 'I killed J.R.' stencilled on them. They were an immediate hit with the public and she had to take on extra helpers to cope with the demand. If a similar catch-phrase comes to mind, then cash in on it.

Bean bags and scratching posts

On a larger scale, bean-bag beds with removable washable covers, filled with polystyrene granules would sell well if the fabric was of higher quality and design than that offered in the average pet shop. And anyone with carpentry skills could make a useful income out of making decorative scratching posts for cats that would fit in, design-wise, with the furniture of an average living room. Or at the luxury end of the market you could make personalised individual dog kennels or sell them in kit form.

Use your talent to try the lucrative pet market, whether it is sewing accessories or making unusual pottery feeding bowls. Try your local pet-shop with samples of your ideas. If they go well, then consider doing mail-order, advertising not just in specialist pet publications but in home and garden magazines as well.

Furniture restoration

Although this is thought of largely as a man's job, many women, too, are now learning this compulsive craft. There is a lot of satisfaction to be had from spotting an item in a junk shop, taking it home and, with the aid of a little tender loving care, turning it into a saleable item.

It's extraordinary how one generation's throw-out becomes the prized possession of the future. Who would have thought that 1950s furniture would become a cult thing to own, for instance? We also view things differently. Previous generations believed that pine in its natural state was an ugly wood, and that it had to be covered up in some way with stain or paint; now there are shops that deal in nothing but stripped pine pieces.

Skills for the job

The skills that you need for restoring furniture are numerous. You need to be good at carpentry, of course, but also be prepared to strip and sand, polish and patch pieces of furniture. You could then go on to learn gessoing and gilding, cleaning and repairing ormolu, and take in items like picture and mirror frames, and mouldings. There are all sorts of other specialised things you could do if you are good at restoration – working with marquetry and veneers for instance. Or you might have an interest in clocks, starting off by merely oiling and cleaning them, and going on to learn about repairs. If you became really proficient, then local antique dealers would be glad to hear about you, too.

There are two ways of making money here: from doing repairs for other people, local second-hand furniture shops perhaps, and from buying pieces at sales, doing them up and re-selling them. Either way you are going to need a workshop in which to do this work, which can be very messy and create unpleasant aromas of things like wood glue, stopping, and acids used for stripping off paint.

An unused garage would be an ideal site, or a shed in the garden. You might be able to convert an attic or the cellar, but you would be better off, in the long run, using an outbuilding for the purpose. You will also need a hatchback car that can take bulky items and, if your business prospers, you might want to invest in a van.

Upholstery

If you are handy with a hammer and nails, and good at sewing, why not combine the two skills and learn upholstery? Most local authorities run part-time classes in this particular trade and you can then augment your lessons with the help of one of the many books now available on the subject.

Although it may take time and practice for you to be able to cover a Victorian button-back chair or chesterfield with velvet, there is a lot of business to be had from people with ordinary upholstered furniture that needs repairing. For it is a fact of life that it's difficult to get something simple, like a bulging arm-chair which needs re-webbing, done in the average upholsterer's shop – which is usually full of antique items. There is often a very long wait before you get your chair back, and the charge will be out of all proportion to its actual value.

So here's an opportunity for you to shine, looking after less than antique furniture, re-covering favourite family settees, dining chairs, stools. If you are also good with your needle, you could offer a set of loose covers for the item at the same time.

To do upholstery seriously, you need a heavy duty sewing machine that can cope with thick fabrics. You will also have to buy special things like curved needles for doing buttoned upholstery, good scissors that again, can cope with heavy fabrics, and a stretcher to help you when you are doing webbing. For lighter items, it pays to invest in a staple gun, and a glue gun for running repairs.

Put a card advertising your services in the windows of local junk shops, and charge by the hour at first until you are confident enough to give an estimate for your upholstering work. You will naturally need to have a room in the house dedicated to this work, with sufficient space to store both furniture and materials.

Repairing china and glass

Restoration of china and glass is delicate work. You must know the techniques thoroughly before you start, and you'll need to work with great care and accuracy. It also depends on what is going to happen to the piece when you have mended it: something that is going to stand on a shelf does not need as strong a glue as it would if it is going to be used. However, modern glues have made the actual process easier than it was.

True china restoration at its highest is an art that can involve complex pinning and moulding, modelling with epoxy resin and painting. Glass is handled in very much the same way as china, but is, of course, more fragile. However, new materials like liquid acrylic resins mean that it is possible even to reinstate the stem of a wine glass. Many colleges and evening institutes now run courses in this fascinating craft.

Bookbinding

Anyone who has mastered the specialist technique of bookbinding should be able to turn this increasingly popular hobby into a business run from home. Restoring and binding old books for second-hand booksellers or doing special tooled leather bindings for publishers of limited editions is painstaking but financially rewarding work. You could also offer a specialist service to private collectors who want their books re-covered, and home in on the 'vanity' market, making sumptuous bindings for açademics' theses and small privately published runs of poems, or diaries.

Picture framing

If you have learned to frame your own pictures competently, then consider setting up a picture-framing service. What the public want is someone who will do their pictures speedily and use attractive, good-looking frames. There are specialist shops in existence, of course, but the average gallery takes a long time to do the work and charges a great deal.

Don't imagine that this is a business you can run from a corner of the living room. The materials you'll need to have in stock take up a great deal of space. Not only will you need a mount cutter, a glass cutter, a mitre box and other tools, but somewhere to keep boards, card, mouldings and half-made frames. Get your mouldings from a good wholesaler, and make up a display board of the shapes, colours and sizes that you can offer. You will also have to invest money in stock to start with.

To get your eye in, make a point of looking round all the smart art galleries to see how they frame the pictures they sell. Remember that the most amateurish or unprepossessing painting can be given a fresh lease of life with the right frame. There are fashions, of course, and currently brightly coloured mounts and patterned frames are very much on the scene.

Once set up, offer your services to local art shops, picture dealers, and, above all local amateur painting groups. Make it your business also to get to know professional artists in the vicinity – a contact like this could result in a contract to frame anything up to fifty paintings at one time for an exhibition.

FINE ARTS

Painting

The life of an artist, like that of a writer, tends to be a lonely one, fraught with setbacks – certainly at first. I'm a fellow artist, so you have all my sympathy! However, if you can appeal to the public, the rewards could be glittering.

Painting is an occupation, thank heavens, that you can do in your spare time. So the best way to become a successful artist seems to be to start gently, rather than giving up your job, painting at home all day, and hoping for commissions.

George had been a keen amateur artist for years, but it wasn't until he retired that he took it up full-time. 'I belong to a local art group and whenever we had an exhibition I sold well, so I thought "Why not take it up more seriously, now that I have the time?"' George's speciality is landscapes of the locality, favourite views. Now he has added townscapes to his portfolio and does a brisk business painting pictures of the historic centre of the town and selling them to locals and to the tourists. 'I have just been commissioned by the Council to do a picture of the town hall,' says George proudly. 'Now I am beginning to make real money.'

It pays to do a little marketing. Be bold about it: at one time I was a completely obsessive painter of sheep. I was sent to Australia on business and noticed that although it was one of the world's biggest wool producers, there were no sheep paintings around. I went into a gallery in Sydney and sold them the idea – one year later I had a one-man show. The idea seemed so novel to them that I appeared on radio and TV and was written up in all the papers – and I sold all my paintings!

Shelagh found that she had an aptitude for catching people's likenesses. Now she runs a thriving business doing portraits for presents. 'I find that people don't particularly like to "sit" for me for hours at a time,' she says. 'So I take a series of colour transparencies of them, and project them on to a wall in my studio. That way the poses are perfectly still!'

As a painter, you need to motivate yourself time and time

again, particularly to finish a portrait. Buy magazines like *The Artist* to give yourself a kick start. Make a point of entering pictures in exhibitions, to give yourself a deadline by which to finish them. I did just that, and got into the Royal Academy summer show! Join a local art group to keep yourself in touch with what's going on locally. Above all look at as many pictures as you can. Haunt art galleries and museums.

If your pictures aren't selling well, just remember that there's a whole spectrum of tastes out there. Think what happened to the Impressionists, the Fauves, and the Cubists when their work was first put on show!

Illustration work

Illustrators are needed for all kinds of published material, from advertisements, posters and packaging to the covers of novels, illustrations in magazines and strip cartoons in comic books. If you've plenty of talent and some training (many art colleges run courses in commercial art and illustration), while waiting for your big break on the art front, consider this lucrative field. You will need to build up a portfolio of your work to show to the outlets that you are targeting. With luck an agent may take you on: look them up in the *Writers' and Artists' Yearbook*. This is an area where you definitely have to sell yourself, knocking on doors, phoning for interviews. But if prospective clients like what you do, and you can produce good work fast, your financial worries are over.

Art restoration

Paintings do not last forever. In fact, the moment they leave the hands of the artist they start to deteriorate. Many are stored for years in unsuitable places – airing cupboards or damp cellars for instance, so it's no surprise that the services of an art restorer are more and more in demand. Painters are not perfect, and the use of the wrong varnishes and pigments, notably bitumen during previous decades means that there are many works in need of repair. Modern paintings are equally at risk: a few years ago one of our museums noticed that the face on a painting on display appeared to be sagging in a curious way. It was literally sliding off the canvas – the artist, apparently, had used too much linseed oil in his painting medium.

If you are already a skilled painter and feel willing to take on the responsibility of handling other people's work, then it might pay you to take a course in art restoration to boost your income. Having once mastered the technique, you could also buy old paintings cheaply and clean them for profitable re-sale. Water-colours, engravings and drawings on paper are also prone to deteriorate especially from 'foxing' – when rusty brown spots appear on the surface. An expert restorer can not only deal with that problem but repair damp stains and tears, making the picture look like new. Then there is always work available as the aftermath of disasters like floods and fires.

Where to learn the complicated art of picture restoration? There are an increasing number of courses offered in this subject. The Courtauld Institute in London, the Victoria and Albert Museum, and major auction houses like Bonham's, Sotheby's and Christies should be able to put you in touch with someone who could help. You could also apprentice yourself, in the short term, to an established restorer.

There are specialist books to be found on the subject (see Help Section, page 195). You will find specialist suppliers of the materials you need, from adhesives and resins to retouching lamps and spraying equipment, in up-market painting magazines.

Glass decoration

Many people come to the art of glass engraving via etching. You certainly need the same talent for precision. Intricate patterns are made on glass in two ways: by etching, that is, working with acid which dissolves the glass where it touches it; and engraving with a wheel or diamond point.

Glass decorating is not for the timid: only lead crystal glass can be properly engraved or etched. If you are capable of doing this (there are many courses available) then you could find yourself putting initials or badges on goblets, even graduating to flowers and other more complicated subjects.

Join the Guild of Glass Engravers (See Help Section, page 195), who not only organise exhibitions but also have a quarterly journal.

CRAFTS YOU COULD LEARN

If you have an artistic bent, then any of the following crafts can be learned from books, magazines or basic training at evening classes. Some of them need precision and attention to detail, others nothing much more than artistic flair.

Calligraphy

The art of calligraphy can be picked up relatively simply from books, if you have the talent for it. Alternatively, there are many courses available in this fascinating craft. The equipment you need to start with is cheap and simple: pens with a range of nibs, and ink which can be bought from art supply shops or stationers. Later on, when you become proficient, you may want to progress to hand-made papers, even vellum. Once you have mastered the craft, there are endless opportunities to sell your skill – doing illuminated addresses, presentation certificates and diplomas. You could also do personalised labels for home-made wines, jams, pickles, to say nothing of greetings cards, and invitation cards. Don't forget that your designs could be cheaply printed too, to make a range of items to be sold in up-market stationers' shops.

Candle-making

Now that it's possible to buy candle-making kits cheaply, the problem of finding materials for this craft has been solved. There is obviously no point in trying to make conventional candles, but personalised ones, multi-coloured kinds, or those shaped like fruits, animals, or birds, would make good sales – especially around Christmas time.

Perfumed candles find a ready market too, so do those with pressed flowers or herbs on the sides. Buy a simple kit and experiment to see if candle-making is for you, then try out your own designs.

Painted furniture

Decorative finishes on furniture are very much in vogue at the present time. You can learn the necessary skills both from books (see Help Section, page 195), and by attending a course on the subject.

Painted furniture has now become very sophisticated, the pieces being rag-rolled or sponged with colour before a motif that has been either stencilled or painted free-hand is added.

If you have an aptitude for this kind of work, and have the space to store furniture, many people would be glad to hear of a service that undercuts the very high prices charged in antique shops. It would pay you to look out for suitable subjects – small cupboards, side tables, and chests, at jumble and auction sales, decorate them and sell them on. Don't forget things for the patio, such as galvanised iron buckets that could be decorated with roses and castles, canal-barge style, with brightly coloured enamels, and window boxes, too.

Artificial flowers

Really beautifully made artificial flowers, whether they are of paper or silk, will always find a market. This is a craft that you can either learn at classes or from books. And if you have the aptitude for it you could make a profitable living.

Don't be afraid to experiment with your materials. Build up a library of flower photographs to work from, and sell your flowers ready arranged in a decorative vase or basket to get extra cash.

Paper making

There are some wonderful, very expensive kinds of hand-made paper on sale now in the shops, some of them art forms in their own right. Paper making, like papier mâché, is a cheap craft to take up, since you have the materials to hand in the house. Although newspaper itself is not very suitable as it is of such poor quality, any other pieces of paper around the house can be pressed into service, and it doesn't matter if they are printed in colour, for it will wash out.

The easiest way to learn paper-making is to buy a kit which explains all. The basic materials – paper, and/or fibres from plants – are shredded, boiled into a pulp, shredded again then moulded into paper.

Later on, you can learn how to make watermarks, and how to press tiny flowers, pieces of leaf, feathers, all sorts of things into the paper – or you could sponge or marble it with colour.

Calligraphers, artists and specialist stationers would all be glad to hear about you. And don't forget to sell your paper direct to the public through craft markets and mail order.

USING YOUR SKILLS IN OTHER WAYS

Writing about it

If you are an expert on something, and have had a consuming passion for it for years, there are other ways of making money from it. Perhaps you could write a handbook on the subject – look around in the shops and libraries and see if there is a need. Then approach publishers who specialise in craft books – Batsford for instance.

Teaching it

Or you could teach – running one-day or weekend workshops in your home. To find customers, advertise in specialist craft magazines or publications like *Country Living*, who have pages of small-ads at the back. You could also approach the local educational authority and see if they need teachers in the subject at the local adult educational college.

SECTION · SIX

Green-finger Ideas

Flowers from seed ... Perennials from cuttings ... Small plants ... Plants for awkward places ... Selling ... Working with flowers ... Dried flowers ... Pressed flowers ... Pot-pourri ... Flower arranging ... Vegetables ... Herbs ... Indoor plants ... Starting a vineyard ... Garden services ... Plants for offices ...Tools and other essentials

IF YOU REALLY ENJOY GROWING THING s, then consider using your garden to turn a private passion into an income. Making money by raising plants, or using them to make into saleable products, beats many of the traditional methods of working from home. It doesn't give you eye strain, it's a quiet occupation that won't annoy the neighbours, and, since you are bending and stretching and working out of doors, it's actually good for your health!

There are many reasons why you may decide to make money from your garden. Mr Unwin of Unwins Seeds, for instance, was a small town grocer at the turn of the century who started off growing sweet peas as a hobby, then turned it into a lucrative business sideline. Now it is one of Britain's major seed companies – and still specialises in sweet peas. At least two award winners who show at Chelsea – Brenda Hyatt, who still uses her back garden in Kent to grow prize winning auriculas, and Simon and Judith Hopkinson who run the gold medal herb farm, Hollington Nurseries – also began in a small way. Even today, the gardening scene is encouragingly full of newcomers following in their footsteps. You will find many of them at the regular shows run by the Royal Horticultural Society at their halls at Westminster.

GROWING FOR SALE: SPECIALISE!

That's all very well, but how can I compete with the giant garden centres, the seed companies, the big growers in this day and age? you may ask. The secret is simple and can be encapsulated in one word: specialise. Companies with a large work force and heavy overheads have to go in for bulk growing and all the expense that goes with it: giant glasshouses that need automatic heating and watering systems, staff that have to be paid at times of year when nothing much is selling. They may even have to buy in plants from other smaller growers – one of whom could be you, of course.

You, on the other hand, can turn your special interest into a fascinating new career by picking one particular type of plant or group of plants, and concentrating on it. You will also be able to devote the time and personal attention to your customers and give plenty of information about whatever you grow, something the larger concerns cannot do. You might also make lucrative profits by following on with some kind of specialist service – more of that later.

There's lots of potential for the keen gardener, even if he or she has only a minuscule plot to work with. But even if you own an acre or so, remember it is pointless and expensive to try and compete with the giant growers who produce plants on a production line basis. However, if you search them out, there are many areas that are not adequately covered.

Growing for sale need not be capital-intensive. Start small, and if your project becomes a real success and you need to expand, it should always be possible to find extra growing space. You can begin with a small outlay and grow at your own pace, ploughing back profits into the business when you can, to help you expand. So, make a start – the worst that can happen is that you will have an extremely well-stocked garden!

Before you start

The first thing to do, is to survey the site, and ask yourself some pertinent questions:

How much usable space have you got?
Size is not as important as you may think, unless you are growing shrubs and trees. With careful planning, thousands of plants can be raised in a season from seed in a mere 10 × 20ft area.

Could you rent more land if necessary?
Although the local authority might not take kindly to you using an allotment for commercial purposes, one good source of extra space might be a neighbour, perhaps an elderly one, who has given up on their garden and would be glad to have someone use it.

What type of soil have you, *acid or alkaline?*
There is no point in flying in the face of nature, so stick to what grows well in your particular pH level. In any case, the type of plant that is happy there will be the kind needed by other people in the locality with similar soil. However, if you are specialising in things for patio pots and containers you can buy in compost to suit yourself.

Have you room to grow early crops or half hardy plants intensively under glass?
If you've inherited a greenhouse or large sun-room, then put it to use for profit to raise indoor plants, bring things on early or to grow delicate flowers. Check out your choice of plants carefully before you start, for some of them may need heat in mid-winter, which could make the enterprise expensive.

Above all, what do you like growing best?
There's no point in specialising in something that bores you, even if it does look like a good financial opportunity. Whether we believe in the efficaciousness of talking to plants or not, they do seem to have an uncanny way of knowing if they are not liked and, therefore, tending to curl up and die.

So, what are you going to grow?

Find a need and fill it, is the formula to follow. But don't attempt to tangle with anything that is being mass-grown in a sophisticated production-line manner. Mushrooms are a case in point. Once a profitable item for anyone with a cellar or suitable shed to grow them in, they are now raised like battery hens and sold very cheaply. However, if you specialised in exotic oriental fungi like the Shitake mushroom, you might well find a market, and at high prices too. The same growing conditions, with the addition of fluorescent lighting and a little heat, could be used for raising African violets instead – money-spinning plants that are amazingly easy to propagate and always popular to sell.

Or you could go for the whole sub-culture of people who collect plants that are rare, not because they are difficult to grow but because they have become temporarily out of fashion and, therefore, scarce. Plant collectors like these are impassioned people who will go to any lengths to find another item to add to their stock, and pay high prices. Kingstone Cottage Plants, is a small home-based enterprise that has become very successful, reviving pretty, historic pinks that had all but disappeared from the big catalogues.

Depending on what you choose to grow, your first year could be mainly spent building up a collection of shrubs and climbers for sale the following spring, and putting out feelers for business; or you may start off right away, growing a selection of quick-maturing plants in large numbers to sell at the market or at the garden gate, and begin to make a profit from the word go.

Flowers from seed

Raising flowers from seed is a quick way of making cash, if you have the patience and aptitude to handle tiny seedlings. A single packet, for instance, could give you 100 plants or more to sell, and a profit of at least 250 per cent. The secret, of course, is to offer something that customers can't find in the local garden centre, and that's where you need the help of the more exotic seed companies (see Help Section, page 195). The initial outlay is small, and as your business grows you'll be able to save your own seed and cut your costs still more. But remember two points here: F1 (that is, first filial generation) and other hybrids never breed true to form, so it is useless saving seed from those plants, and it is now an offence to sell seed that is not approved by the EEC regulations – so check out the varieties first (if the particular seed is not listed in seed catalogues, contact the Ministry of Agriculture, Fisheries and Food).

Perennials from cuttings

Growing on perennials from cuttings can also give you quick returns and good profit. You can also easily get fifty or more off-spring from one 'mother' geranium plant during the course of a season, and sell them on individually. You can charge more if you've chosen something really unusual, so there's a great deal of potential there.

Check out the market carefully to see what's readily available, and what is thin on the ground, or missing altogether from sale. Look in *The Plant Finder* (which should be in your local library) and it will show you at a glance which of your chosen plants are readily available. It might be unusual ornamental shrubs, or ready-shaped topiary pieces in tubs. Or it could be something specialised you're interested in, such as cacti, bonsai, or scented-leaved geraniums (pelargoniums). There could well be an interest in your area, too, in unusual new varieties of bedding plants which you could raise from seed. Bear in mind, however, that the easiest, cheapest plants to grow in our climate are the hardy ones. Anything that can't stand frost may cost you money, if you have to overwinter it.

Small plants

It's a well known fact that the average garden is tending to shrink in size, so another good opening would be to specialise in dwarf versions of familiar plants, for almost everything in the herbaceous border now comes in mini-sized versions. If you search the seed catalogues you will find you can raise compact versions of things like Michaelmas daisies and golden rod, even stumpy delphiniums and knee-high sunflowers, but you'll never see them on sale in garden centres. Small can certainly be lucrative: a grower in the West Country has build up a very successful business planting up true miniature gardens in troughs, and supplying plants to customers who want to make their own. He has now followed it up by writing a book on the subject which he sells direct to his customers, maximising his profit.

Plants for awkward places

A good way to turn a disadvantage into potential profit, if your garden is less than perfectly placed, is to specialise in plants for similarly awkward conditions. Your own patch may get little sun, for instance, which gives you a perfect opportunity to specialise in shade-loving items, featuring plants like hostas and, surprisingly, begonias and busy Lizzies which can all take these conditions. Or, if you have a dry sunny garden that tends towards drought, why not grow plants with silver foliage which will thrive in these conditions – artemisias, verbascums and lavenders for instance, and supply them to people who are similarly placed.

It would pay you to sell by mail order if you're running a specialist operation like this to capture a large number of customers. Many people are already running successful businesses this way. There is a woman in Hertfordshire, for instance, who has a thriving business selling ground-cover plants to people who hate weeding, and a man in Essex who specialises in a huge range of ivies, with leaves of all shapes, sizes and colours, which are ideal for covering ugly walls. (See also below.)

SELLING YOUR PLANTS

First survey the scene and see where the potential is. You may decide to sell direct to the public. There are many ways of reaching them: at the garden gate, for instance, if your setting is suitable – though you'd need to make sure that cars could pull off the road safely and that you were not contravening any local regulations. Car boot sales, which are proliferating and now seem to be held almost every weekend throughout the country, are a very good place to sell plants. Keep your eyes open for posters advertising such sales as you drive around, and look, too, in the local paper. Then your local town may have a weekly market, where, for very little money, you could take a stall. Or organisations like the Women's Institute may hold regular fairs.

Charity days

Open your garden to the public on charity days and have plenty of plants to sell. It's a good way to attract customers who will come back again and again to buy if they like what you have on offer, and are able to see it growing on site. Be sure that the plants have really informative labels and that you are on hand to answer questions, and give advice.

Mail order

Mail order, as I have said, is another good idea if you have a particularly specialised range of plants. So, as you build up a list of regular customers, it might pay you to have a simple typewritten or computer-set catalogue. Meanwhile, you can make a start by putting simply printed leaflets through letterboxes, and perhaps take a small display advertisement in the local paper. The word usually gets around, on the garden front, if there is someone in the locality selling something that is interesting or unusual, for people like to discover new plant sources, and you won't have long to wait.

Later, as your business grows, you could apply for a place at the Royal Horticultural Society's shows (see Help Section, page 196) and even eventually make Chelsea. Don't forget that there are flower shows throughout the country all through the summer, not just the large ones like the Southport show, but smaller local ones, including county shows, where you know you will find fellow gardening enthusiasts, and where you will be able to exhibit and sell your plants.

Look around locally. Don't disregard small tradespeople: florists, garden supply or hardware shops and greengrocers, for instance, who tend to lose out against the garden centres and supermarkets. Many of them would not interest the big growers who, if they sell on a large scale, tend to supply huge wholesale markets. You, on the other hand can provide unusual foliage, flowers and indoor plants for florists, bedding and vegetable seedling plants for hardware stores and greengrocers to sell in boxes out on the pavement. Many interior decoration boutiques like to sell exotic indoor or window-box plants in unusual containers. If they don't, why not suggest it to them? Gift shops, too, might be interested in smaller plants like African violets or cacti in attractive pots (look for containers at local auctions, and in junk shops.) Then, on the food front, you might find success with special herbs, salads and exotic vegetables for local restaurants which find it difficult to locate small, regular quantities elsewhere.

WORKING WITH FLOWERS

If you love flowers, the scope for selling them at all stages of their development is tremendous. You can start with baby plants raised from seed, and go on to full-grown perennials for the border. Then there are cut flowers, edible flowers for salads, dried flowers, pressed flowers for pictures and cards and, finally, pot-pourri made from fallen petals.

Themes

The best way to attract custom is to theme your flowering plants, growing them in special collections: flowers for cutting, flowers for scent, cottage garden plants (an increasingly popular purchase) or curiosities – all-green flowers like the tobacco plant nicotiana ... bells of Ireland, *Alchemilla mollis* (lady's mantle) and the chic euphorbias – *E. characias wulfenii*, for instance. Or black and white flowers might appeal to you – there are black versions of a number of flowers, from hollyhocks to violas and pansies, if you look carefully through the seed catalogues, and there are plenty of white ones to choose from too.

One-colour collections

Another idea would be to offer chic one-colour flower collections in plant form: all pink, white, yellow or blue, or mixes of pastels. Again, the place to look for ideas is in the catalogues. These same flowers could be grown on as cut blooms for flower arranging clubs – a thriving market once you have made the contacts – or for florists. But check that your chosen specialities *do* make good cut flowers; not all plants do, of course.

Or you could soon become an expert in one particular flower that interests you. Here again the field is wide open, especially for half-forgotten flowers – the Victorians were besotted by violets, for instance (which must surely be due for a come-back) and even raised tiny standard plants from the larger varieties for table decorations.

Dried flowers

Dried flowers for winter displays can be a money-making idea and can fetch high prices – provided you look for unusual things to grow. Surprisingly, almost anything will dry, from hydrangea heads to the ethereal gypsophila, and don't forget ornamental grasses which are so easy to raise. You need a warm dry place from which you can exclude sunlight to get the best results with flower drying. Bunch them together, using an elastic band rather than string (it will then shrink as the stems do, and still hold them in place), and hang them head downwards. Flowers with large heads can be 'posted' through the holes in chicken wire stretched over a frame.

Get books on dried flowers out of the library to see what can be used in this way, and experiment. Don't just stick to simple arrangements; go for garlands, posies, other shapes and sizes, and remember that the drying process for many of them can be speeded up by using a microwave. (See Help Section, page 197.)

Pressed flowers

Buy or make yourself a simple press, and if you have the artistic talent you can enter the magic world of flower pressing. The results can be made into attractive pictures, or mounted on stiff paper for unusual anniversary cards. One of the largest and most successful companies in this country selling pressed flower cards to the National Trust is run by a family team – and started as a hobby done by the wife in her spare time.

Penny first became interested in pressing flowers when she took over a derelict garden in Cornwall. 'I wanted some way to preserve them,' she said. So she created a series of totally new pressed flower pictures, some of them with an abstract appeal, pasting her flowers on to rich fabrics like velvet.

Now, with several best-selling books on the subject to her credit, she divides her time between her pictures and her writing.

Pot-pourri

It has to be said that the shops, even supermarkets, are currently inundated with pot-pourri items, many of them quite unpleasant, basically nothing more than coloured wood shavings that are cheaply perfumed. But there is still a market for the real thing if you use subtle blends of natural perfume and give your pots eye-appeal – dry some flower heads in silica gel, then scatter them on the top. It pays to hunt out old traditional recipes – a 17th-century pot-pourri, for instance would have great tourist attraction.

Flower arranging

If flower arranging appeals to you, you could take your growing
one stage further and expand into wedding and special occasion
arrangements with a difference, made from home-grown flowers. Another idea might be to do interesting pieces for table
decorations at dinner parties: low arrangements, so that the
guests can see each other over the top of the blooms. Be sure to
check out the flowers you grow for this purpose carefully – you
don't want to waste time with anything that wilts easily or has a
short blooming span. And you would find a greenhouse, conser-
vatory or polythene tunnel an advantage to protect delicate
petals from the rain.

  If the idea of decorating with flowers appeals to you, it might
pay you to take a course in floristry. It needn't necessarily cost
much; check with your local adult education college. Many
local authorities run floristry courses as evening classes. There
might be the potential, too, to give talks on flower-growing or
flower history to local clubs, when you could sell plants to your
audience at the same time.

VEGETABLES WITH A DIFFERENCE

Although it would be foolish to go for field crops like potatoes
and cabbages, vegetables can be profitable to grow if you choose
the right type. If you have plenty of space and prefer to stick to
the traditional carrots, onions and sprouts, however, because
that's what you've always done, there's still a gap in the market
for the organic grower if you are prepared to dispense with
chemicals. Well-grown fruit and vegetables raised in an entirely
natural way fetch high prices, not just in the greengrocer's but at
health food shops, too. And you could probably build up a
round of direct deliveries to regular customers.

  If you do have the space in which to do it, consider growing
gourmet vegetables for maximum return: individual baby cauli-
flowers, colourful ornamental but still edible cabbages and

unusual types of potatoes like the French ratte. You have several opportunities here: you can approach top class greengrocers, build up your own customers and deliver direct to them. You could also build up a business with local speciality restaurants, growing things to order, provided you are able to offer a reliable service. Courgette flowers, for instance, if you can grow them, are much in demand by top chefs – they stuff the blooms with forcemeat for exotic starters. Edible flowers, too, such as the marigold, pansy and nasturtium, to name just three, could be grown and marketed in mixed packs for the restaurant trade.

There is a booming market for unusual salad crops. The ubiquitous radicchio and other colourful lettuces are not worth your attention because they are now found everywhere, ready-bagged in supermarkets for instance. But individual-sized ones like 'Tom Thumb' and 'Little Gem' might well find a market. And you should be able to make a sizeable profit in the autumn by sowing late exotic Oriental salad crops such as mizuma greens, straight-sided Japanese spring onions and edible chrysanthemum leaves, which mature much more quickly than European salads do, and can withstand cold weather. Extend their growing season, too, by covering them with cloches as winter comes.

Unusual and exotic vegetables

There's no doubt that unusual and exotic vegetables can be profitable, even if they are simply miniature versions of things like sweet corn, beet. So do your own market research, look and see what the classier food stores are offering (watch the vegetable counters at Marks & Spencer and Sainsbury's for new ideas), and grow and sell the same produce from seed for small local shops. Surprise them, too, with items like the 'spaghetti' marrow which they won't see elsewhere; it looks just like spaghetti when cooked and opened up. Or supply unusually shaped squashes and pumpkins. It's a good idea to offer your customers recipes to go with them – look in American magazines for ideas on the latter items.

Sowing in succession

To keep up your supplies and avoid disappointing customers, it is vital to sow your vegetables in succession so that you can crop them on a weekly basis. Lengthen the growing season with the help of glass – cold frames constructed with old windows for lids are another useful aid. Sowing every week or ten days will also avoid gluts, when you have difficulty in getting rid of all your stock. On a small basis, however, you could offer a range of frozen vegetables direct to regular customers.

With plenty of space to hand you could also try growing old-fashioned hard-to-find items like medlars, quinces, and alpine strawberries that can't be tracked down in the shops. If you had a prolific harvest you could consider turning them into jams and pickles (see Section Three, page 63).

SMALL-SPACE HERBS

If your growing space is on the small side, a good way of making money is to specialise in herbs, since you can pack so many in a small space and they fetch relatively high prices. Herbs are very accommodating plants for they prefer a soil that is not too rich, though it should not be waterlogged. And provided they get whatever sun is going they are relatively free from pests (which hate their smell) and diseases.

Away from the obvious mint/thyme/sage beat, there are more than a hundred unusual herbs to choose from, and they are useful in so many ways not only as small plants for sale but in their dried form too. People never seem to tire of visiting herb gardens and love to hear about the history of the plants, so if you've the ground to spare, it is well worth while planting up, perhaps an Elizabethan knot garden edged with clipped wall germander, santolina or box and filled with specimen plants so that would-be customers can see what their purchases will look like when fully grown.

Ready-planted herb pots make best-selling gift items – keep the plants well manicured, and try painting an ordinary clay pot white with acrylic paint for maximum effect. Also try packaging your herbs in white china soup tureens, or other small containers, so that they can be sold to go on the dinner table – add a small pair of scissors and the guests can garnish their own salads. Herb standards sell well. Make mop-headed mini-trees from myrtle, rosemary and small-leaved sage and grow them in little pots. A selection of herbs to use with the barbecue – rosemary, oregano, sage and so on – would sell well growing in a suitable metal container for outdoors.

Historic herbs like the bible leaf plant (costmary) and rue – used to repel witches – could be planted together in a container with a story to tell. Another original idea would be to sell the herbs for each sign of the zodiac (a good astrology book will tell you which ones they are). Then you could have a tub of plants in all silver and gold – for instance, the curry plant, golden marjoram, southernwood and variegated lemon verbena.

If you have a knack of growing basil from seed – and the greenhouse in which to do it – there are fifteen different varieties to try, none of which ever reach the shops at the moment – holy basil, black-ruffled basil, lettuce-leaf basil and aniseed basil are just a few that you can find in specialist seed catalogues, and they make handsome plants to sell for the garden border as well as on the windowsill near the kitchen sink.

Herbs into gifts

Maximise your profits and use up unsold plants by turning your herbs into gift items. Herb vinegars, even mustards are very easy to make, and dried herbs can be turned into culinary aids such as bouquets garnis – but bear in mind that you then have to comply with the *Food and Drugs Act*, and have to ensure that the leaves are clean and insect free. Decorative bouquets of mixed cut herbs for the kitchen also sell well. Customers can either put them in water for decoration or hang them up to dry. On the aromatic front, dried herbs can be used for sleep pillows, potpourri and lavender bags.

The medicinal market

There's the medicinal market too: herbalists, aromatherapists and other people working with aromatic plants find it difficult to get supplies locally, and would be glad to know about you. Local restaurants and gourmet food shops would appreciate a service in cut herbs if you can offer a regular supply, high quality and the more unusual things – garlic chives instead of ordinary chives for instance, fresh tricolour rather than plain green sage, and unusual variegated mints.

INDOOR PLANTS

When you come to analyse the indoor plant scene, the possibilities are endless. Get away from the simple plant in a pot and you can let your imagination run riot. You could offer ready-planted indoor water gardens for instance, bowls with miniature water-lilies in them. You could specialise in indoor trees like the *Ficus benjamina*, or hanging fern, and flower balls using fuchsias, *Begonia semperflorens* and the Boston fern.

Then there is the world of miniature plants: dwarf African violets planted in king-size brandy glasses, or species daffodils and tulips for indoor bulbs with a difference. Then there are the miniature evergreens like the baby junipers, and other tiny plants in a decorative terrarium.

You could offer indoor pots of herbs, or a herb hanging basket to hang over the sink. You could even plant up an indoor wildflower garden, edged with moss. In America, there is a woman who makes a living out of selling indoor cat lawns – freshly grown grass on wooden trays for the family moggy to be used indoors or on terraces or balconies.

The keen gardener with greenhouse space to spare should raise indoor plants for sale, for many exotic-looking items are amazingly easy to propagate. Keep away from the Christmas cactus, poinsettia, and indoor azaleas, of course, because the market is well covered. But some others are worth trying: mother-in-law's tongue (sanseviera) and the African violet (saintpaulia), for instance, can be reproduced from pieces of leaf, and geraniums (pelargoniums) are among the easiest plants to take cuttings from. If you offer these plants grown in unusual containers instead of the standard pot, you will attract sales. Seed of exotic indoor plants sown in the spring should give you good-sized plants to sell at Christmas time.

Almost all indoor plants need some heat, but some, like cyclamen, for instance, can be raised in cool conditions. In order to compete with the large multiple stores which now sell indoor plants in large quantities, you need once again to specialise. Cacti and succulents if they are in attractive containers can make good sales, so can air plants which seldom see their way on to the supermarket shelves.

Offer something special to your customers: large containers with a number of different plants growing in them, for instance, or a selection of plants like the aspidistra, which can manage on low light levels. Plants that it is almost impossible to kill – mother-in-law's tongue for instance – would make a good sales line to sell to beginners. Indoor climbers such as the philo-dendron, trained up bamboo frames, would make another un-usual item. Better still would be indoor topiary – tiny-leaved ivies and helexines trained over wire or oasis shapes to make pyramids or spheres. You could even try for little animals: an elephant cut out of oasis, for instance, would need four ivy plants to start with, one planted at the base of each leg, secured in place, as they grow, with fine hairpins.

A VINEYARD

I can tell you from personal experience that starting a vineyard is a costly business. Not only do you have to invest in the vines, but there is also a question of posts and wires, rabbit-proof fencing, and machinery not just for tending the plants but for making wine.

However, if you have a large area of suitable ground – ideally a south-facing slope – it is undoubtedly a fascinating thing to do. But you are talking in terms of acres – a quarter of an acre will yield, on average, one bottle for every day of the year. Don't be under the illusion that people will pay large sums of money for the wine you make – there is still a prejudice against 'home grown'. But if you have the surroundings and premises where you can run your vineyard as a tourist business – showing people around, then giving them a wine-tasting, and possibly feeding them too – you will make more money.

Robert and his wife bought an old railway station, and converted it into their home and wine-making premises. 'We soon found that running a simple vineyard wasn't worth while,' says Robert. 'But when we started offering tours and serving teas, we began to make money.' They now also have 'gourmet' dinners from time to time that bring in even more cash. For help and advice, join the English Vineyards Association (see Help Section, Page 196).

GARDEN SERVICES

If you can offer some sort of service as well as the plants, you are carving out a new, unique section of the market that will bring you in more money.

Instead of simply selling the plants, why not offer to plant them in as well? You could also have a business selling ready-planted hanging baskets, maybe renting out some of them to pubs and shops with a follow-up maintenance service. Your local garden centre might well be interested in taking them for sale, too.

Or you could become a patio specialist, offering ready-planted tubs and boxes, grouping the plants according to colour themes, or giving them, say, a tropical look by mixing a yucca with other spiky looking things. You could grow the plants in cellulose liners which would make them lighter to transport. Then they could be dropped straight into the customer's container. And you could have ready-planted baskets of bulbs for spring – ragged-edged parrot tulips, for instance.

Growing on plants in a special way can raise extra money. Take topiary, for instance. An ordinary garden shrub will only reach a certain ceiling price. But if you hang on to it a little longer, train it into a spiral, a cone, an animal or a bird, then you can command a large amount of cash for it. For example, small topiary animals in pots cost between £100 and £200. Training is a matter of twisting and clipping, usually on a metal frame, but you can make quicker ones by covering the shape with climbers. Evergreens are obviously best, but a flowering dog, covered with a rapacious clematis like *Clematis montana* would be a fun item to sell, and would reach a high price, as do daisy trees in tubs, made from *Chrysanthemum fruticans*, or standard geraniums in tubs, which take about two years to mature.

Plants for offices

Another service that would be well worth trying is supplying small local offices with either cut flowers or indoor plants on a regular basis. You could also offer to install and maintain containers like window-boxes for them. There are many firms specialising in this kind of work in the big cities, but only for giant business conglomerates. You could canvas small firms like solicitors, accountants, insurance agents, even shops and suggest you look after them on a regular basis.

Plant sitting is another idea for making money on the side. You could either take in and look after house plants for people, or visit their homes to water them when the family are on holiday. The same could be done for garden plants. A customer might have a special flower bed that needs an eye kept on it, for instance, for few people have automatic watering systems. And there is nothing more discouraging than coming back from holiday to find that, in your absence, things you have grown lovingly from seed have wilted and died.

Jobbing gardeners are thin on the ground now, and if you're good at general gardening work there's no doubt you'd have no difficulty in finding employment. You could offer your services in a different way, perhaps – specialising in keeping people's front gardens up to scratch, or becoming a pond specialist, or looking after lawns.

TOOLS AND OTHER ESSENTIALS FOR THE JOB

Which tools do you need to get started? It depends, of course, on what kind of gardening you're planning to do, but it always pays to buy the best quality you can. There is nothing more irritating than a spade or, on a smaller scale, a trowel, that buckles and breaks, and it's a false economy too. If someone wants to give you a present, get them to buy you one with a stainless steel blade.

A greenhouse is a major investment but necessary if you are growing half-hardy plants. However, if you have the space, a polythene growing tunnel gives you far more space for your money. Machine tools like cultivators and hedge trimmers can be hired at first, to cut down on capital expenditure.

Growing pots: keep a lookout for second-hand ones, which you can also sometimes find on rubbish dumps, but they will need cleaning thoroughly before re-use. Remember when buying that square pots take up less space than round ones and tend to be more stable when being transported around in a car.

Growing compost will be another basic need. Don't be tempted to get by with ordinary garden soil which is full of diseases, weed seeds and pests. But shop around a little – sometimes grow-bags from the supermarket work out cheaper than the traditional potting compost, and the soil is perfectly adequate for grown-up plants.

Then there will be labels – plus a rainproof pen with which to write on them.

Trays

Later you may want purpose-made wooden trays but at first you can take your plants around in boxes cadged from supermarkets or greengrocers' shops.

Plugs/pop-out cells. If you're raising from seed plants which have a high selling price, or are tricky to transplant, it will pay you to sow them in plugs of compressed compost or tiny individual pop-out cells. That way they have minimal root disturbance. However it would be an expensive proposition for annuals, for which you are not likely to get a huge return. These need to be sown in conventional seed trays. Larger-seeded plants can be sown in discarded yoghurt or cream pots, or milk cartons with the tops cut off. Get into the habit of saving them and, at the same time, saving money.

Cellophane/wrapping paper. If you're selling cut flowers, then you'll need to invest in cellophane and wrapping paper; if you're making herbal products, you will need bottles and jars.

A hatchback car, or one with a capacious boot will be a necessity for collection and delivery, so you can load up with plants, or sacks of compost and fertiliser. (It will probably pay you, too, to devise some wooden containers to keep the pots securely in place, especially when driving round a bend.) Later, if the business thrives you might consider a small second-hand van, fitted out with special racks.

Space considerations. Whether you're starting from seed, taking cuttings or dividing up mature plants, make sure that you have the space to store the increased population. Hardy plants pose no problems, they can simply sit outside. But when you are raising from seed you need to plan, and sow in succession, to avoid traffic jams. Otherwise you could find yourself with more fledgling tender plants than you can get into the greenhouse.

Once the plants have reached a marketable stage and, in the case of half-hardy varieties, all danger of frost is past, put them in a standing out bed to make room indoors for more. The bed is best made by digging over a patch of ground and then putting a layer of pebbles on top for drainage.

What Next?

As you become more experienced and more successful, be bold, set your sights on the European community too, homing in on our reputation as the best gardeners in Europe. In France, for instance, there is a growing craze for *le jardin anglais*, filled with old-fashioned cottage flowers which are quite difficult to track down. If your French is good enough, you could offer an instant garden design service over there, taking your plants with you now that new regulations make it much easier to take plants abroad.

Working with People and Animals

The beauty business ... Hairdresser ... Keep-fit instructor ... Colour consultancy ... Child minding ... Play groups and nurseries ... Activity groups ... Fostering ... Working with the elderly and the handicapped ... Teaching languages, cookery, computer skills, music, dancing ... Tutoring ... Pet sitting ... Running a kennels or a cattery ... Breeding pets ... Quarantine ... Pets' parlour ... Dog obedience classes ... Agility training ... An animal model agency ... Keeping bees, Poultry, Goats

IF YOU'RE USED TO WORKING IN a salon, clinic, nursery or day centre, in fact any of the 'people' professions, there's often no reason why clients should not come to your home instead, for the service you provide. That way you are in control of your own appointments, and can give more personal attention to your clients.

THE BEAUTY BUSINESS

The health and beauty business: hairdressing, manicure, beauty treatments and massage, and chiropody, can all be carried on from home if you have a room to spare. Some local authorities ask for planning permission if you are using part of your house for this purpose, others have by-laws to cover hairdressing, ear-piercing and electrolysis. The best way to find out is to make discreet enquiries about this.

Certainly, one room of the house will have to be designated a treatment room, even if it leads a double life, night and day. And you will have to provide somewhere for people to hang up their coats and somewhere for them to sit while they are waiting. They may also want to use the lavatory, of course.

Hairdresser

Lisa has been hairdressing from home for two years now, ever since she became tired of commuting to a London salon. She finds plenty of customers in the locality who are happy to use her services – particularly handicapped or elderly people – who find it almost impossible to park in town, or mothers with small babies in tow.

She started off with a small nucleus of regular customers from the salon, and has then built up her clientele through recommendations. If she needed more, she would advertise in the local paper. Already armed with the basic hairdressing equipment, all she had to buy was a small portable hood dryer (from Argos) for those people who didn't want their hair blow-dried. She gets her shampoos, conditioners, perming lotions, and sprays from a local wholesaler.

'The hours are unsocial, of course,' she says. 'Everyone seems to want to have their hair done when they come home from work or at weekends, but it's good if you have a child to look after, for instance, because you can fit your work around that.' Occasionally, Lisa will visit someone in their own home to do their hair; if they are ill, for instance. She then charges extra, to cover her travelling time and expenses.

Lisa finds the temptation to be too sociable with her customers – sitting eating cake and drinking cups of tea – can also eat up her working time. 'I have another rule,' she says. 'Never invite men that you do not know to the house for a haircut, and don't put cards advertising your services in the wrong kind of shop windows or you may find yourself mistaken for a prostitute!'

Extra cash

Make extra cash (out of any form of beauty service) by selling products to your customers. Whether it is body lotions, nail care kits, or special shampoos and conditioners, your clients will be in an amenable frame of mind to buy. Contact lesser-known cosmetic companies or those that sell by post or by parties and become a local distributor. If you are interested in herbs and herbal preparations, you could make up your own skin-care products and sell those, making an even larger margin of profit.

Costings

Don't forget, when setting your prices, in addition to obvious expenses such as shampoos and sprays, to cost in such things as laundering of towels, extra electricity for use of hair dryers, heated tongs, massage machines, constant hot water, and perhaps the central heating kept on all day. All these items could eat into your profits and leave you worried that you don't seem to be making as much money as you should. Apart from your basic equipment, don't forget to buy an appointment book to keep by the telephone or in your pocket. Names and times noted on the backs of envelopes tend to get lost! A cordless phone you can carry around with you might be useful, so that you don't have to dash away during treatments.

Keep-fit instructor

In the age of the 'personal trainer', anyone who is qualified to run keep fit classes could make money giving individual lessons at home or catering for small groups. But you need to know exactly what you are doing, for the wrong exercises could result in pulled muscles, all sorts of aches and pains, and trouble from your customers. So take some up-to-date training first (see Help Section, page 197). Unless you are working with sophisticated equipment like a Nautilus machine, all you are likely to need is a cassette player for music, perhaps a simple wall bar or items like the Step, basically an upturned plastic box, for working sessions on the hips and thighs.

Keep an eye on the fitness videos that come on to the market. It's worth while buying them to see what the latest thinking is on the subject. Remember that you will need somewhere for your clients to change, and possibly shower afterwards.

Colour consultancy

Working as a colour consultant is a popular idea that has come to us from America. It works on the premise that both men and women can be grouped into one or other season of the year, according to the colour of their eyes, hair and skin. That being so, they need to pick from the appropriate season's palette of shades when buying their clothes and, in the case of women, also the make-up that harmonises with this particular palette.

The organisation trains suitable people to qualify as consultants, and backs them up with promotional material, cosmetics, accessories and fabric swatches. There are also several books you can read on the subject, including *Color Me Beautiful, Color for Men* and the *Color Me Beautiful Make-up Book*. If you are good with people and have maybe worked in the fashion business – perhaps as a sale assistant, then consider training to be a Color Me Beautiful Image Consultant. For further details, see Help Section, page 198.

WORKING WITH CHILDREN

If you like looking after, or working with children, then you have a whole host of activities that you could do from home. Baby-minders, as such, are subject to certain regulations now, so you need to check carefully before taking in other people's children on a regular basis. However, running the occasional informal playgroup, when you relieve mothers for a few hours while they go shopping, is a good way of making money by looking after children. You are also providing a much needed service to the community, for groups like this are few and far between.

The ways of making money from child care are endless, as the suggestions that follow show.

Child-minding

If you are going in for any form of child-minding, any idea of keeping the house pristine goes out of the window. It's sheer common sense to put away any objects that you treasure, especially breakable ones. The same goes for precious carpets. And if you are the sort of person who would freak out if a small child scrawled on your wallpaper you have two choices: either dedicate one room in the house as a play room and furnish it accordingly, or find some other occupation!

Your main 'clientele' will be children under the age of five, who are not eligible to go to a council nursery and are too young for school. However, you might find that there is a service needed looking after older, school-age children during the gap between the time when school ends and when their working parents return home.

Child-minding is understandably regulated by the social services department of the local council, with whom you will have to register. They will visit you to make sure that the premises are suitable and that you can provide activities to keep the children happy and occupied, indoors and out. You will also be asked to have a chest X-ray if you haven't had one recently. This rule is strictly enforced now that there is an increased incidence of TB in this country.

Margaret, who has a small son and daughter of her own, finds that looking after another two or three children doesn't seem to increase her work-load unduly. 'In fact, it keeps my own two occupied,' she says. She has to keep an eagle eye on the small group, of course, which precludes her doing housework at the time but she does find that she is able to knit while she does so. And she is earning extra money that way, making sweaters and cardigans for children, which other mothers are eager to buy.

'My initial outlay was very small,' says Margaret. 'I don't

take babies, only toddlers. My children have so many toys that there are plenty to share around. Apart from that, I simply invested in a roll of wall lining paper for them to draw on, some modelling dough and some felt-tip pens, plus unbreakable mugs and plates for their mid-day break. I'm lucky in my clients, they've become my friends. In fact, one of them does my shopping for me when she goes to the supermarket!'

Being houseproud and child minding do not go well together, and Margaret cheerfully admits that her house is beginning to look rather battered. 'Fortunately, my husband doesn't mind; he's too busy fiddling with his motorbike in the shed to notice the mess.' Margaret's husband has, however, built her a large box-cum-seat which she keeps in the hall. At the end of a session, all the toys can be flung into that and shut out of the way.

Playgroups and nurseries

If you're a qualified nursery nurse, or have plenty of experience in working in this field, there is always a need for playgroups or private child nurseries. To do this, you need first of all to register with the local social services, and you may find that you have to take on help. There are strict rules regarding the ratio of children to adults. There are several organisations that can help you in setting up, the British Association for Early Childhood Education, for instance, and the National Childminding Association (see Help Section, page 198).

Emergency numbers

Needless to say, when you take on someone else's child you must make sure that you have all the basic information you might need. Emergency telephone numbers: of the child's doctor, and of both parents, for instance. Also, background information like the child's date of birth. Find out about favourite foods and what he or she will not eat, and whether the child is allergic to any substance. If the child is very young you need to know at what time of day he or she takes a nap, and whether he or she is fully potty trained. If you are going in for child care in a serious way you may need to invest in some equipment. Remember that car boot and garage sales are the places where you can pick up second-hand cots, prams, and other items at reasonable prices. Look, too, in the small ad columns of your local newspaper and give-aways.

Activity groups

You may not want to go in for child minding on a regular basis, but if you have organisational or artistic skills, and a large enough house and garden, think in terms of running holiday or weekend activity groups for school-agers, another way of making money and helping harassed parents at the same time. Activity classes at the weekends would be popular. And anyone who can keep children occupied on a regular basis during the school holidays would be sure to make good money. Cash in on your particular skills – painting and clay modelling groups would be one idea, or you could start a small theatre club at your house, where children could meet, dress up and act out plays they have written themselves.

Fostering

Taking in children whose parents cannot or will not look after them themselves is one of the most worthwhile jobs in the field of child care. But it could not and should not be considered a way of making an income. It is a vocation, taking all the patience, understanding, love and care that you can muster, often with tragic or difficult charges.

Iris has fostered eight children over the years, as well as bringing up four of her own. 'It's not easy,' she admits. 'We've had our problems over the years, but we got through it all. They've all left home now but I still think of them as my family, and they all keep in touch. Three have got married and have children of their own, and I like to think that being in a loving home, as they were, has helped them in bringing up their own families.'

If you feel that the commitment of bringing up a foster child might be too much, but would like to help, consider fostering on a short term basis. Or do what I did and have a child who is in care for holiday breaks. We were living on a sailing barge when Arthur came to stay with us. The local child-care officer came to inspect us first and took it all in her stride. We then had him for several summers until he was happily adopted.

WORKING WITH THE ELDERLY AND THE HANDICAPPED

If you are prepared to look after a frail, elderly person in your home, then many people would like to hear about the service you are offering, particularly now, at a time when so many basic care services are being cut back. Technically, they would rate as lodgers, but you might well need some basic training in home nursing (see Help Section, page 198).

Taking in elderly relatives on a short term basis, to give their carers a break, is another way of using your home creatively, particularly if you have nursing skills. Tact and patience and the ability to listen would be needed here.

You could also provide the same kind of valuable service for the mentally or physically handicapped, taking someone perhaps for one day each week, to relieve the relatives who normally look after them. Contact your local health services, who might well know of people who need your help.

TEACHING

If you've a particular skill, why not capitalise on it by communicating your expertise to other people? Whether it is an art or craft, an aspect of music, or a language, someone out there would like to learn from you.

Languages

Our well-deserved reputation for being bad at languages, seems to be shaming more and more people to brush up their French, German or Spanish, if only with a holiday in mind. Going to evening classes is all very well, but most of us fall by the wayside sooner or later.

If you have language skills and could make learning fun, then you could corner the market in individual tuition or with small groups. Advertise your services with something extra about them. For example, you could run short courses in shopping, buying a house (with a run-down of all the legal requirements), motoring, or sight-seeing in your chosen language. The very good BBC language series on videos and audio-tapes, available from main bookshops and record shops, would be a great help in composing lessons. You could also contact local firms and offer to give individual tuition to executives who have to travel abroad.

If you are dealing with groups, don't make the mistake of taking a mix of beginners and those who are relatively proficient. People who are struggling with the basics usually feel totally demoralised in a situation like this, while the advanced speakers will be bored. Give them a simple test then sort them out into stages. Don't just preach at them, make the lessons lively. They could, for instance, act out buying vegetables at a market stall with props from the kitchen; or practise buying clothes. Keep your own vocabulary up to date with the latest buzz-words by subscribing to one or two foreign magazines.

Teaching English

Teaching English as a foreign or second language is worthwhile work. In the first case, you could be dealing with anyone from a group of businessmen needing a crash course, to school children over in Britain on holiday. English as a second language is needed by immigrants, often Asian wives, who are trying to get to grips with basic things like shopping, visiting the doctor, and the school, and you could provide a valuable service helping them with this.

Tact, a sense of humour and a great deal of patience are needed to do this work. You can train to get official qualifications, which later will enable you to work in a college (see Help Section, page 197). It is a great advantage to have videos to show, to liven the lessons up. You could show home-made ones, of yourself going out shopping, or catching a train, for instance.

If you are teaching English as a foreign language (or, indeed, if you are teaching a foreign language to British nationals), and you have the space, you could augment your income by running total immersion weekends, having small groups and making them speak nothing but the language you are teaching them. If you have spare rooms, have them to stay and earn yourself some extra money from these paying guests.

Cookery

If you have a spacious, decorative kitchen and a particular skill in, say, cake-making and decorating, cordon bleu cooking, or making some kind of ethnic food – curries for instance – then why not capitalise on it in another way. Small cookery classes in any of these subjects would be popular among local foodies, particularly if you held them during the day to fit in with school hours.

You're likely to need more than one cooker, unless you are simply planning to demonstrate. It is relatively simple to install one or two small, second-hand electric cookers or, depending on the type of food you're doing, table-top rings. If you have something really interesting to show, then you could charge a high price for your classes. Consider linking your classes with something else. If you are a keen gardener, for instance, you could have a herb day, with a mixture of growing and cooking herbs – and even sell herbal products and plants on the side.

Computer skills

If you are confident that you know all there is to know about your particular brand of computer, consider running one-day familiarisation courses for other souls who are still struggling with their how-to-use manuals. Or give individual lessons. Owners of popular but complicated machines such as the IBM, the Macintosh and the Amstrad would gladly pay to find out how to get the best out of them.

Music

Music teachers have almost always traditionally worked from home and have to put up with unsocial hours since most of their pupils will want to come after work or after school. If you have the necessary grades to teach singing, or a musical instrument, then the family will appreciate it if you can designate a relatively sound-proof room for the purpose, as stumbling scales can become tedious background music. Enquire from other teachers in the neighbourhood for rates – pretend you want lessons.

If you have the space to do so, letting a room out to a small local group – a quartet, for instance – to practise in, could bring in more cash.

Dancing

Dancing lessons for tinies could be given from home, if you have a room that is large enough to take them. Dulcie, who had been a ballet dancer until a foot injury ended her career, decided to take up teaching when she needed cash.

'My husband died suddenly, I was left with this huge house that I couldn't sell, and enormous heating bills' she said. 'So I thought "give dancing a try" and it's been an enormous success. People prefer to come to my home, rather than go to a draughty church hall. I'm lucky that I was able to convert an old Edwardian billiard room into a practice space, and I have a friend who comes and plays the piano, although I use a tape recorder a lot.

I've just started a dance class for teenagers, using pop music and it's a hit – they've got so much energy they need to get rid of!'

George and his wife, both retired, are keen ballroom dancers, specialising in Latin American steps. They make a useful income giving private lessons. 'Not everyone wants to go to a class,' says George. 'We get all sorts of people – like a woman who was going on a cruise, hoping to find a millionaire! She knew that there would be an opportunity to do lots of dancing, and she wanted to brush up her steps. Because we are both gold medalists we also get a lot of people who need coaching for competitions – we feel very elated when we see one of them on TV!'

Tutoring

If you are an ex-teacher who has kept up with the intricacies of the National Curriculum and the latest details of Common Entrance then your services would be welcomed by worried parents who feel their children need help. Coaching school pupils who are falling behind in their studies is another way of using tutoring skills. Notes pinned on boards in local schools, leisure centres, colleges, public libraries or a small-ad in the local paper will usually bring in customers.

Consider, too, the possibility of working for correspondence colleges, marking and grading papers. This is a particularly good idea if you don't particularly want to have people in your home. (See Help Section, page 199.)

Remedial teaching is not only well paid but also a very rewarding thing to do. To see a backward child finally learn to read or to count, or a dyslexic teenager to spell, gives both pupil and teacher a very special kind of pleasure.

WORKING WITH ANIMALS

If you are one of those people who like animals to the extent that you actually enjoy caring for them on a regular basis, then there may be some aspect of working with pets that you could do from home. But unless you are thinking in terms of just taking in a few, or looking after small creatures like rabbits, or hamsters, the neighbour factor comes into play. There is no point in contemplating running, say, a kennels or a cattery unless your house is situated in the kind of surroundings where the noise and the smells will not obtrude.

Pet-sitting

Small-pet sitting could be a useful way of using your home. Many families have a menagerie of guinea pigs, gerbils, terrapins, fish tanks which cause problems when they want to go away. And taking in small-scale creatures like these should not pose a problem – unless you have a cat who would regard them as a possible dinner!

You may, however, find yourself handling say, a hamster for the first time. The RSPCA can come to the rescue here. They have a series of useful leaflets on virtually all kinds of domestic pets, and are always willing to give advice (see Help Section, page 199). Be sure to find out exactly what you are in for. A friend of mine answered an advertisement for an animal sitter and found herself confronted by a Vietnamese pot-bellied pig!

If you have a paddock at your disposal, and the necessary know-how, you could take in the occasional large animal, a pony or a goat, for instance, or a pet Jacob's sheep for short periods of time. Taking in birds, too, while their owners are away is relatively simple and profitable. Charge extra for large or messy specimens. The mynah bird for instance eats nothing but fruit and spatters it both inside and out of its cage in the process. A parrot that is used to being let out could also be rather a trial.

Dog-sitting and dog-walking on a regular basis could bring in useful money. Catherine didn't think ahead when she fell in love with a small dachshund puppy. She thought it would be happy at home while she was out at work but days of agonised howls soon alerted the neighbours, who called in the RSPCA. Now she drops the puppy off each day with a friend who acts as a dog-sitter – a job that, perhaps you could do, too.

While cats are too independent to come to stay with you without being caged, many people would be grateful to know – and pay for – someone to call in and look after their cat on a regular basis when they go away, checking the house at the same time.

Convalescent pets

Another opportunity for anyone who has had some training would be to take in and look after convalescent animals whose owners are out at work and are unable to give them round the clock care. Get in touch with your local vet – the chances are that he does not have the space to keep animals that are recovering from an operation or illness and would be glad of your services. Make sure that you get full details from the owner of the animal's habits, and favourite foods, to make sure you can give it tender loving care during convalescence.

Running a kennels or a cattery

It goes without saying that you must be passionately interested in animals to run a kennels or a cattery. And you need, of course to live in an isolated place with no chance that there will be complaints from the neighbours.

This is not a career to be entered into lightly, and will inevitably involve a hefty financial investment. But, with so many people constantly on the move these days, whether for holidays or business, taking in their pets can be very profitable.

You will need planning permission to set up a proper kennels in your garden. And if you are going to breed or board animals on a large scale then you'll need to get a licence under the *Animal Boarding Establishments Act*. There is a fee for this, which varies according to which local authority you deal with. Get in touch with the Environmental Health department for details. They will want to know the size of the quarters where the animals will be housed, what material they are made of and how they are heated and ventilated – so converted out-buildings might not be accepted. They will also want to know such diverse details as where sick or infectious animals are to be kept, where the water supply is, what arrangements you have for storing food and what kind of exercise area you are planning.

You will not only be looking after your charges but cleaning and exercising them as well. Charge extra for looking after animals that are on heat, or likely to be so, since they have to be kept well away from not only the males that you are boarding but also dogs or cats in the neighbourhood that might stray in.

Since you're going to be out of doors a great deal, it would pay you to invest in a cordless phone that you can carry around in your pocket. You are required by law to keep meticulous records of the animals – their arrival and departure dates for instance.

For your own sake, you need to have a large appointments book or card index system, in which you can note the details of each animal, its name, likes and dislikes and the dates when it had its vaccinations. If you are in any doubt about the condition of the animal you are going to take in, ask for a health certificate for it. Your peak times will be during the summer holidays and at Christmas. This is when you will find yourself needing some help. Ask around, and advertise in the local paper.

Make a friend of your local vet: not only will you need him or her in cases of illness among your charges, but he or she in turn will recommend you to clients and probably let you put a card up on the notice-board in the surgery. You will also need to take out specialised animal insurance from a specialised company (see Help Section, page 199). You could make some useful extra cash in commission, by selling pet insurance policies to owners who come to you with their charges.

Breeding pets

If you have a pedigree pet – a perfect poodle or a prize-winning Siamese, for instance – it is perfectly permissible to earn pocket money by breeding from it at home. It is only when you decide to invest in other animals or keep more than a reasonable number of the offspring for breeding purposes that you might fall foul of the regulations.

If breeding dogs or cats on a large scale is a possibility in the future, check out whether or not you will get the planning permission to do so. It could be that you will have to move! However, breeding small pets or goldfish is a more containable career. When Avril's small son bought a hamster, he was told that he had to be personally responsible for the animal's welfare.

'You can guess what happened,' says Avril. 'Within a fortnight I found myself having to clean out the cage and remember to refill the water bottle.' Feeling that the hamster was lonely on its own, she decided to buy it a partner. Now she makes a useful income by breeding them and selling them on to pet shops. If you are going in for small-scale breeding in this way, you would make more money out of dealing with rare animals, or going for something that is fashionable – dwarf rabbits for instance.

Quarantine

A more specialised way of looking after animals, is running a quarantine premises. This is a lucrative long-term business since, despite attempts by the European Economic Community (EEC) to change our law, all animals that come in from abroad – not just dogs and cats but pets like hamsters and gerbils too – have to be kept in quarantine for six months.

Before you can begin to look after animals in quarantine, you not only need planning permission but you also have to get authorisation from the Ministry of Agriculture, Fisheries and Food (see page 191 for address). For approval, you will need to be able to provide at least ten segregated compartments for the animals, with separate exercise, feeding and drinking facilities.

You also have to have an approved veterinary surgeon (that is, a member of the Royal College of Veterinary Surgeons) to inspect the animals once a week, and your premises will have to be inspected by the local divisional veterinary officer before you start. You, yourself, can be protected against rabies by a simple vaccination – though rarely, if ever, does an animal go down with this disease.

Your charges will come to you from the port or airport of entry, where they have been handed over by the owners in a special container. They may well be distressed and disoriented at first, and that is where your special talent for caring for animals will come in.

You can get a good regular income from quarantining, though beware of bad debts, as the odd owner here and there might renege on payments for their charge. Looking after animals like this, long-term, means that you build up a special relationship with them and, probably, with their owners too.

Leaving a pet in someone else's care for as long as six months is an emotive thing, and owners will want to come on regular visits. Since they may have travelled some distance, you'll need to have facilities at least for giving them a cup of tea. You could, of course, make extra cash by having them on a bed and breakfast basis from time to time. Devoted owners being the way they are, you'll have to keep a look out for the possibility that they may attempt to kidnap their pet!

A pet's parlour

Many kinds of dogs – airedales and poodles for instance – and certain long-haired cats, need constant grooming if they are to look good. This involves shampooing, brushing and occasional clipping. If you already have some of these skills then it would be easy to learn the rest and set up an animals' beauty parlour. This would be best sited in an outbuilding – perhaps you could convert your garage. And it would be necessary to run in plumbing for a sink, a water heater and some electrical points. Items such as brushes, clippers, scissors, shampoos could all be bought from a wholesale pet shop supplier. And to bump up profits you could sell accessories like leads and collars and other items that you could, perhaps, make yourself.

This kind of business is only suitable for someone who is good at handling animals who never, at the best of times, enjoy being given a bath. But if you have worked, say, as a vet's receptionist in the past, if you have dogs of your own that you groom on a regular basis, then it is worth considering as a profitable side-line to pet-sitting or running a kennels.

Dog obedience classes

While no one has ever succeeded in controlling a cat, if you've discovered that you have the knack of training dogs – perhaps acquired from taking your own animal to classes – then running dog-training sessions is another thing you can do from home. Enquire from the Kennel Club (see Help Section, page 199), about training courses. You will need a large lawn, paddock, or space to take several animals at a time, and you should charge for a course of, say, six lessons at least. Remember that you are training the owners as well as the dogs, and your ability to get on with and ultimately control people is as vital as your skill with dogs. Some local authorities demand planning permission for this kind of exercise, usually if you have to give lessons in a building such as a barn. Enquire at your local council office before you start up.

Advertise for customers, ask to put a card up in your local vet's waiting room – he or she should be delighted, as a trained animal is more docile to handle. Try also to get an article written about yourself in the local newspaper; that's the best way to attract people.

Agility training

If you find that you have a flair for training dogs, then you go on to coach them for agility, too, which is the canine equivalent of show-jumping. This is a relatively new field: it was founded some twelve years ago by a group of enthusiasts who wanted to train their dogs to do something different, and decided to combine the elements of obedience, sheepdog working trials and horse show jumping. It has now become such a success that clubs are springing up all over the country, and is cult viewing whenever an event is televised.

To run agility classes, you need a large amount of space – a field or paddock for instance – to take the equipment, which consists of a series of jumps, 'walls', suspended tyres, and frames. It is a long-term project to think about, since training to be a teacher in agility is based on experience, rather than a crash course of lessons. The best way to start is to take your own dog along to a training evening. Most people who try it find this sport is totally addictive, and there's no doubt that the demand for classes far outstrips the supply. For more details contact the Kennel Club, or one the many local clubs around the country (see Help Section, page 199).

An animal model agency

Another way of making money from an interest in animals is to set up an animal model agency. Years ago I was pregnant and stuck at home temporarily. I'd been working on *Vogue* magazine, where one of my jobs was to help the fashion photographers. At that time, there was a fashion for using animals in pictures and I found myself, at one time, trying to get hold of twelve greyhounds in a hurry. So when I retired for a while I decided to start supplying cats, dogs and other small animals for photography and films, perhaps even the stage. I had contacts among photographers, of course, but otherwise I was on my own.

I seldom if ever saw either my clients or the pets. I bought a copy of the magazine *Our Dogs*, rang the breeders who advertised puppies for sale in it, chatted them up, did the same thing for cats, and gradually acquired a card index of animals. Then I contacted theatres, stage companies and television people, offering them my services. I scarcely ever left the house, I would be phoned and asked for, say, a Jack Russell. I would then contact the owner, tell her where and when to take the dog, charge the company and pocket a commission. The enterprise was a huge success, especially after the BBC came down and interviewed me, on one of the few occasions when I saw some of the animals I supplied – with disastrous results. There was a dog-fight in my kitchen.

I found the job a great deal of fun. If the project sounded interesting, I would take the animal along myself – that's how I

came to share a dressing room with a monkey working for a
BBC show. Another time, I got a donkey jammed halfway up the
stairs to a Soho photographic studio.

There are a number of professionals in the business now, but
there is still room if you specialise in some way – perhaps in
birds, reptiles, something different. Find your charges in the
specialist magazines, as I did. Most animal agencies are
London-based, so, if you are out of town, local photographers
might be very grateful to hear of your services.

Keeping bees

There are more beehives per square acre in central London than
in any other part of Britain – that strange fact shows that you
don't need a great deal of space to take up beekeeping.

However, to do the job properly, you do need a large garden,
especially if there are small children in the family, when the bees
will have to be kept well away from them. And you will need to
lay out quite an amount of cash first in equipping yourself. First
of all you will need your beehives. You can find these advertised,
second-hand, from time to time, in specialist magazines. But
they are not a good buy, since they will need to be sterilised
before you can use them, and it is difficult to tell, as a novice,
how many years' use you will have from them. So my advice is to
buy new ones. Then you need things like a bee-proof veil and
boiler suit, a smoker and equipment for extracting and storing
the honey.

Bee-keeping is not just a hobby, more a way of life. Expect to
get stung; even the most experienced beekeepers are, from time
to time. It may be that you are only interested in getting your
hands on the end product, that is, the beeswax and honey. If so,
then consider buying in supplies from a local beekeeper rather
than raising them yourself.

If you are starting to keep bees from scratch, with no previous
experience, enlist the services of someone from your local Bee-
keepers Association – they have clubs all over the country.
You'll find, too, that there are all sorts of organisations who will
be happy to help you (see Help Section, page 200). You can

also attend courses on the subject, covering essential techniques such as controlling a swarm.

Buy your colony of bees in the spring. Don't be tempted if you live, say, in the north of England, to buy bees that are used to the milder south; stick to a colony raised in your own area. Having installed them, hope for a fine summer, for your output of honey, rather like that of grapes, depends on good weather.

Encourage your bees to stay put by planting the garden with flowers that they enjoy. Many cottage garden annuals and perennials: marigolds, candytuft, nasturtiums, Canterbury bells and golden rod will encourage honey production. Among the herbs that bees love best are marjoram, lavender, horehound and hyssop. Even if you live in or near town, some typical suburban trees and shrubs are attractive to bees: buddleia, honeysuckle, pyracantha, and cotoneaster, for instance. And if there is a lime tree in the vicinity, so much the better.

Unless you happen to live in the country, and are bordering a field of clover, or your house is situated in the midst of heather, the honey you produce will be a mélange of nectar from different sources. Beehives are very often situated in orchards for a good reason: June is the month when blossom is still difficult to find and the nectar-rich flowers of apple, cherry, pear and plum trees provide a welcome source of food. If you lack fruit trees in your garden, then plant plenty of catmint, which starts flowering in June, is rich in nectar and goes on blooming all summer. Bees need attention from time to time, mainly in the winter, when they have to be fed with a syrup made from sugar if the temperature dips.

Most people love honey, and you should find a ready sale for your product. Bear in mind, however, that as a food, it has to comply with certain standards for weight and labelling (see Help Section, page 191). Honey is usually sold in 8oz (250g) or 1lb (500g) screw-top jars, or occasionally plastic or waxed paper tubs. Then the combs can be melted down or rolled to make beeswax candles. You could try your hand at making and selling beeswax polish for furniture or even cosmetics. A selection of honey-based beauty products, from face masks to moisturisers and day creams, would go down well and might even be sold in local health food stores or through the post via health magazines. Try places like your local hairdresser, too, for outlets for your products.

Poultry

At one time, raising free-range eggs was a profitable business, but now so many large firms have muscled in on the market that unless you have a guaranteed outlet it is not really worth while. However, it could be that duck or goose eggs might find a place in a local delicatessen or health food shop. And if you can bring yourself to kill and dress the birds, you may find a market for them, too. You will need to provide clean, dry shelter for them and fencing against foxes, which are even on the prowl in suburban areas these days. You will also need somewhere to store feeding stuffs.

Breeding ornamental fowls could be a profitable way of working with poultry. To find out more about this specialised area, contact the Domestic Fowl Trust (see Help Section, page 200).

Goat keeping

You don't need a great deal of garden space to keep goats, and the profit from them can be quite high if you sell milk (a surprisingly large number of people need it, because they are allergic to cows' milk). Goats do, however, need an area to themselves, as the 'jokes' about them eating clothing off the washing line, branches off trees – any piece of greenery they can get hold of – are quite true. Given an exercise space and a dry shed or pen, however, they will live alongside you quite happily. Always buy a pair, for they are gregarious animals and will protest loudly if alone. The cheapest way to start, if you are prepared to wait, is to buy 'maiden' nannies, that is, kids, and take them to be mated when they are of age (see Help Section, page 200), for information on clubs and societies that can help.

You will need to provide a continuous supply of drinking water for your goats, and plenty of greenery and hay for them to eat. This can include household scraps, but be careful about garden waste for things like tomato and potato foliage would be poisonous to them. Don't contemplate goat-keeping unless you have some sort of backup help, or you will be tied to your home. The routine of feeding and milking must go on week in week out. You must also keep a watch out for foot and mouth disease, an infection to which goats are very susceptible and which has to be reported immediately to your local officer from the Ministry of Agriculture.

There are few restrictions at present on the sale of dairy products made from goat's milk, though your local Environmental Health officer may take an interest in what you are doing. Expect to get between five and six pints of milk a day per animal. It does not need to be pasteurized, although in its raw state it will not keep very long. Goat cheeses, whether fresh or matured, always make a good sale, especially if they are attractively presented, rolled in herbs such as chives or savory or wrapped in fig or chestnut leaves.

Contact local specialist places such as health food shops and delicatessens to find a market for your products. If space is limited, consider keeping angora goats which produce mohair.

The Help Section

Helpful organisations ... Income tax ... Insurance ... Taking a partner ... Limited companies ... Trade marks and patents ... Raising cash ... Your business plan ... Other sources of loans ... Useful publications and addresses

HELPFUL ORGANISATIONS

PROVIDED YOU ARE WORKING by yourself, for yourself, you don't have to register with Companies' House (see below), but you do have to pay your own National Insurance and you will have to notify the Income Tax authorities.

The Citizens Advice Bureau If you're starting up any kind of enterprise, your local **Citizens Advice Bureau** is an invaluable free source of help, saving you hours grappling with red tape. You will find the nearest one listed in your telephone directory.

There are many other sources of help. **The Greater London Business Centre** has a list of useful contacts throughout England, Scotland and Wales. Ring them on Tel: 0800 222 999.

If you live in the country, the **Rural Development Commission** (formerly called Cosira), 141 Castle Street, Salisbury, Wilts SP1 3TP, Tel: 0722 336255, has offices throughout the country. For a small charge you can get technical or business advice from their experts.

Giving yourself a name

What name are you going to trade under? Remember that the name you choose needs to be something that will tell complete strangers instantly what you have to offer. It should also be something that they can remember, usually a short, catchy name rather than a long one. Avoid names that are difficult to pronounce. Your new name should go with the kind of business you run – don't make it sound too up-market (or too down-market), or you may frighten off customers. It should say what you are – tinker, tailor, candle-stick maker or whatever.

You can use your own name or make one up, without tangling with too much red tape. I can call myself plain Hazel Evans without any problem. If I call myself The Evans Brain Factory or make up something fancy like The Think Tank, for instance, I still don't have to register, but it is up to me to make sure the title is not being used by anyone else, or that it sounds or looks like another trade name. You can look up existing business names at Companies' House (see below). There are some names that are considered to be overstepping the mark. If I called myself Queen Hazel or a Royal writer I could be in trouble.

Regulations SI 1685//1981S1 and *1653/1982* from Her Majesty's Stationery Office (HMSO), list special business names that need the approval of the Secretary of State. They are mainly those that sound as though they're connected with officialdom or royalty: names like Windsor, royal, etc.

If you use a name that is not your own, the law says that you must show the name and address of your business both on the premises at which you work, that is, your home, and on your stationery. And you must give it in writing, on request, to any customer or supplier who asks for it.

If you are at all perplexed by the legislation, then call at **Companies' House**, at 55 City Road, London EC1Y 1BB (no queries answered by telephone or letter), Companies' House, Crown Way, Maindy, Cardiff CF4 3UZ, which *will* take telephone calls (Tel: 0222 388588) or Companies' House, 102 George Street, Edinburgh EH2 3DJ – write or call personally.

Ask for a copy of the Department of Trade's leaflet: *Notes for Guidance on Business names and Business ownership*.

Income tax

Once you switch from being employed by someone to working for yourself, you change your status as far as income tax is concerned. You are now self-employed and come under Schedule D, which has many advantages, for you can charge many more items as expenses, and get tax relief on them. If, however, you are working as an outworker for one supplier you may not qualify. If you are not absolutely sure, about this, ask yourself:

- Am I solely answerable to any one company in my work?
- Do I personally have to supply absolutely all the equipment which I use for my work?
- Am I in charge of my own hours of work?
- Have I got my own money invested in the business, or have I borrowed it against my own collateral?
- If the business makes a loss, am I solely responsible?
- Do I decide how the business is run?

If the answer to all of the above, except the first question, is 'yes', then you definitely qualify for Schedule D; if not, then you need to seek advice from your local taxman.

If your affairs are going to be complicated, and particularly if you are due to pay VAT, then an accountant is invaluable. But don't think you can hand him or her a shoe-box stuffed full of papers – you will still have to do your own basic accounts for him or her to handle.

There are several tax publications worth reading before you actually set up in business by yourself. The Inland Revenue have three useful leaflets: *IR57 Thinking of Working for Yourself? IR 28 Starting in Business*, and *IR56 Employed or self-employed?* If there is any problem over getting copies from your local tax office, contact the **Inland Revenue** at Somerset House, London WC2R 1LB, Tel: 071 438 6420. The following things can usually be charged against tax:

- Heating, lighting, cleaning your workplace,
- The cost of your raw materials e.g. stationery.
- Business telephone calls.
- Postage.
- Subscriptions to professional organisations.
- Subscriptions to trade magazines and newspapers.
- Payment to helpers.
- Advertising and publicity.
- Travel expenses and hotels, when travelling on business.
- Proportion of the running costs of your car.
- Interest on business loans and overdrafts.
- Business insurance.
- Repairs and maintenance to equipment or work premises.
- Depreciation on equipment.

Insurance

One of the first things you will need to do, when you start working from home, is to change the terms of your insurance. If you neglect to tell the insurance company that you are running a business on your premises your policy could be invalidated, should things go wrong.

Most of us sign a statement when we take out a policy on the house, saying that it is used purely as a residence. If you are then trading from your house and some purely domestic incident happens – say the washing machine overflows and ruins the kitchen flooring – the company could refuse to pay up if they found you were working from home without their knowledge.

In many cases they won't ask for an extra premium – if you are using a word processor for instance or something that does not materially change the status of your house. However, they may refuse to insure the equipment itself (that has happened to me), and you then have to shop around for separate insurance to cover the items concerned. Ask someone you know who is already running a business from home. The areas you need to check are:

Public liability

If people are coming to your house on business, or if you are employing anyone even on a casual basis, you must be covered for this. Otherwise if they, say, fall down the stairs and injure themselves, you could be in trouble. If you are making some product that could in some way harm a customer – perhaps a meal that could cause food poisoning, then you need to cover yourself for product liability, too.

Theft

If you are storing other people's possessions in your house while they are being repaired, or if you are carrying stock of some kind, then you need to make sure you are covered for theft and damage. The insurance company may want to send someone to inspect the premises and make sure that they are reasonably burglar-proof.

Fire

If you are taking in paying guests, letting part of your house or using materials that could be flammable, it may be necessary to take out extra cover against fire.

Car

If you are delivering or collecting things in any quantity in your car, then you should tell your insurers. Otherwise, if you have an accident and the vehicle is found to be full of goods, the terms of your insurance might be nullified.

It never pays to be mean over insurance. After all, you can charge the cost against income tax. And if disaster strikes and, say, the house catches fire, you not only lose your home but your workplace too, and therefore your income.

If you are actually employing people in your home then you need to know about the Employer's Liability (Compulsory Insurance) Act. The Health and Safety Executive, Baynards House, 1 Chepstow Place, London W2 4TF, Tel: 071 243 6000, has a guide to the Act. They also have other leaflets to give you more guidance on health and safety at work.

National insurance

Leaflet NP 18 from your local Social Security office gives guidance for the self-employed on national insurance. *Leaflet N127A* gives special information for people with small earnings from self-employment.

Taking a Partner

As a sole trader, you find yourself feeling like Atlas from time to time, with the whole world on your shoulders. So it's not surprising that the idea of setting up a partnership is very seductive. You would then have someone else with whom to talk over your problems. They will also presumably inject some capital into the business and, by the same token, take on some of the debts. In fact, the law says that partners are 'jointly and severally responsible'. 'Severally', alas, means that if your partner should run off to the Caribbean, you would have to settle any of his or her debts, even if you had no idea what they had been running up.

Think long and hard before taking on a partner or partners. Are you absolutely in accord over the way the business should be run, over future plans, over money? Many a friendship has foundered when the pair concerned went into business together. If you are absolutely convinced that you can make a go of it, then get a legally binding contract drawn up, stating exactly what will happen if one of you wants to pull out, and dealing with minutiae like who pays the bills, who writes out the cheques.

Partnerships are subject to the same Income Tax regulations as sole traders, so you still get more tax relief than if you were employed. And you do not have to register partnerships with the Department of Trade and Industry.

A Limited Company

It sounds impressive to say that you are running a company. But the very word 'limited' highlights the snag – few people will give a brand new company credit, because they are justifiably afraid they may not see their money again. So, in practice, there is very little difference between setting up a company and working for yourself – banks and other concerns will insist you put up personal collateral, give personal guarantees, probably mortgage the house if they are giving you a loan.

A limited company must have more than one shareholder, however small the holding. Someone has to be designated company director and someone company secretary. The paperwork increases dramatically. You need to submit audited annual accounts to Companies' House. You also lose some tax advantages, as you have to either pay yourself a salary or a dividend. The only real advantage of having a limited company is that although you may end up penniless if it fails, you cannot personally be sued for bankruptcy.

Limited companies are really only for high-flying businesses that are obviously going to expand. It costs money to set one up, but you can save by buying an existing company that is no longer trading, and can be bought 'off the shelf'. To do this, you need to find a companies' registration agent (look in *Yellow Pages* for one).

Get more information about forming a company from the **Companies' Registration Office**, Companies' House, Crown Way, Maindy, Cardiff CF4 3UZ or, if you live in Scotland, from The Registrar of Companies, 102 George Street, Edinburgh EH2 3DJ

Trade Marks and Patents

If you want to use a particular symbol, then you should consider registering it as a Trade Mark. This gives you the sole right to use it on whatever goods you are producing. If you are providing some sort of service, for example, catering, and want to use a special symbol, then you can register it as a Service Mark.

Contact the **Trade Marks Registry** at The Patent Office, Concept House, Cardiff Road, Newport, Gwent NP9 1RH, Tel: 0633 81400 (or their London number, Tel: 071 438 4700), requesting their free booklets called *Applying for a Trade Mark* and *Applying for the registration of a Service Mark*. These set out clearly what you need to do and how much you have to pay for the advice of the Registrar. If you are convinced that you have invented a process or machine that is completely new and of wide use to the trade, then you should patent it to protect yourself.

To help guide you through the patent jungle, there are professional patent agents. You should find some listed in your local Yellow Pages. If not, get in touch with the **Chartered Institute of Patent Agents**, Staple Inn Buildings London WC1V 7PZ. They have information sheets on many aspects of patents and trade marks, too. If you decide to go it alone, write to **The Patent Office**, at the same address as the Trade Marks Registry, above, for an application form and information on how to use it.

RAISING CASH

Even though you may be able to start your business off without help, there may come a time when you need extra cash. This situation often arises when you are beginning to do well, the orders are coming in, but you have a 'cash flow' problem: you need to buy supplies and there will be a time-lag before your customers pay you.

If the money is to be used to add on to your premises or take on staff, ask yourself first, 'Do I really need – want – to expand?' It is all too easy to get swept away by grandiose ideas without thinking of the long-term implications. If you are working away happily by yourself, with a full order book, expansion may be a happy thought. But how good are you at management skills? You're likely to find yourself dealing with staff, accounts, taxes and deliveries rather than doing the creative work that attracted you in the first place. Many creative people have fallen into that trap.

Rapid expansion is not always a good idea. Remember all the successful names that mushroomed, then went down in the Thatcher years. You don't want it to happen to you. Ask yourself, 'Is the potential there on a long-term basis, or am I fooling myself? Could I quickly saturate the market?'

If you decide you do need money, the obvious place to approach is your local bank. But banks have currently got a bad name for encouraging people to borrow then coming down on them like a ton of bricks when times are hard, often forcing them out of business.

The responsibility for borrowing, however, is yours. Always follow your basic instinct and don't be tempted by smooth-talking salesmen to buy more, or borrow more than you actually need. That new car can wait until the business can afford it.

Over many years' experience of starting businesses, I have found city branches of banks more laid back, more willing to loan large sums or money or listen to innovative schemes than small ones. After years in the hands of small-time managers, I am now happy to be a totally insignificant customer of a big London bank that lends out millions overnight and is therefore not particularly interested in me.

My thoughts on the subject are now borne out by the experience of a friend of mine who owes her local small-town bank some money and is being virtually persecuted by them – to the extent that she is unable to get on with her work. On the other hand, I have to say that a really good local manager who knows the area and is on your side can be a useful friend. He might suggest people who could help, even put business your way.

The bank may offer you an overdraft to help with the day-to-day purchases you need to make. This is the most flexible way to borrow, since you only take out what you actually need at a given time, but always bear in mind that the bank can call the overdraft in without notice at any time if they turn unpleasant. The other method of borrowing is by a formal loan which may have to be covered by a personal guarantee by you. You may have to lodge share certificates with them, or you may even be asked to re-mortgage your house. The advantage of a loan over an overdraft is that the former is fixed. Usually the bank will open up a loan account for you, and you then pay it off at a fixed rate over a year or more.

Currently, the government is operating a **Loan Guarantee Scheme** with the banks, to help small businesses. To see if you qualify, ask about it at the local branch of your bank.

Before lending you money, your bank will want to see a business proposal from you showing where you are at and where you are going. Indeed, the more business-like you can be the more likely you are to get money. So don't turn up with figures scrawled on the back of envelopes. Have a proposal properly typed. Making a business plan is a good exercise for anyone working for themself. It gives you a bench-mark to see where you are going.

Your Business Plan

The bank will want to know what the structure of your business is, whether you are the sole proprietor and whether you employ people. You should also include a brief CV showing what training you have had and what a splendid employee you have been in the past! It should also include:

• **What you need the money for, and how it is going to be used.**
A bank manager friend once told me that half the people who come to him for a loan haven't really worked out what it is actually for. They just feel that they need more money!

• **A cash flow forecast**
This will give details of when and how the money will be coming in and what needs to go out.

• **A budget for the year ahead.**
So that the bank can see where its money will be going.

• **The potential market for your service or product.**
The more you can give in the way of local population trends, and sources of customers, the better.

• **A survey of the competition.**
Competition is a double-edged sword. On the one hand you

have to battle against them to get business. On the other hand, the very fact that they exist shows there must be a market for what you are doing.

Try not to get disheartened if you are turned down. Remember that the bank manager is answerable to his employers if he lends money to people who go bankrupt or cannot pay it back. By all means look for other sources of money. However, don't be tempted to borrow by buying things on your credit card unless it is on a strictly short-term basis. The annual percentage rate of interest – APR – on all credit cards tends to be astronomical.

Other sources of loans

The financial pages of newspapers often contain tempting advertisements from companies offering loans, or willing to invest in your business. Consult your accountant or solicitor before entering into any arrangement of this kind.

Friends may offer you money. In that case, think it over very carefully (see partnerships) and if you do decide to accept, get your solicitor to draw up a proper agreement. Ask yourself: do they want a share in the company, and if so, how will I feel about giving up total control? How much interest are they expecting, and can they call the loan in at any time without notice? You can sell shares to investors on a temporary basis – ask your accountant for details of the Share Buy Back Scheme.

If you are buying capital equipment, it's possible that a carefully thought out hire purchase could spread the cost over a period of time. Again, ask your accountant.

If you do need capital and can't get it from the bank, it's worthwhile reading a booklet from the Department of Employment called *Finance without Debt*: a guide to sources of venture capital which may help. Check, too, whether there are any regional development commissions or enterprise boards who could help. These are being set up and stood down so rapidly at the moment that it is impossible to list them here. But your local town hall or Citizens' Advice Bureau should be able to tell you of the current situation. At the time of going to press, for instance, there are Training and Enterprise Councils throughout the country which can advise you on setting up your business, help you with training and even pay you a small sum per week as you do so. These have been set up to help the unemployed, so to qualify you must have been out of work for at least six weeks, and be planning to set up a new business.

USEFUL PUBLICATIONS AND ADDRESSES

General

You should be able to track down some of these publications via a secondhand bookseller or your public library.

Get *The Small Business Guide to Advertising*, free of charge, from Thomson Directories, 296 Farnborough Road, Farnborough, Hants GU14 7NU.

Willings Press Guide and the *Writers' and Artists' Yearbook* list magazines, publishers and journals in this country, *Willings Press Guide* also gives circulation figures and advertising rates. The Post Office can deliver leaflets for you; you can also take advantage of their freepost services. Ask at your local post office for *Inland Compendium*, a booklet giving details of these and other services.

Section two: making your house work for you

At the time of writing you can take in up to £3250 per annum in rent, tax free, under the Government's Rent a Room scheme. For details, get *Housing Booklet 22: Letting Rooms in Your Home*, from the Department of the Environment, PO Box 151, London E15 2HF.

Planning

If you are going to make obvious alterations to your house, particularly to the exterior, you may need to contact the local authority planning department.

Taking in tourists

English Tourist Board
Thames Tower
Black's Road
London W6 9EL
Tel: 081 846 9000

Northern Ireland Tourist Board
St Anne's Court
59 North Street
Belfast BT1 1NB
Tel: 0232 231 221

Scottish Tourist Board
23 Ravelston Terrace
Edinburgh EH4 3EU
Tel: 031 332 2433

The Wales Tourist Board
Brunel House
2 Fitzalan Road
Cardiff CF2 1UY
Tel: 0222 499 909

Putting up signs

Ask to see *The Town and Country Planning Control of Advertisements Regulations* (1969) at your local council offices.

Useful publications

Letting rooms in Your Home, a Department of the Environment booklet, available from your local Citizens Advice Bureau.

The Fire Precautions Act, a Home Office guide, available from HMSO.

Renting and Letting (Consumers' Association *Which?* publications).

Solicitors' stationers often have model lease forms.

Section three: cooking from home

Food regulations
The Ministry of Agriculture, Food and Fisheries
Room 303A, Ergon House
Smith Square
London SW1P 3JR
Tel: 071 238 6550
has a Consumer Helpline to answer queries on food matters. Ask them to send you their booklet: *Success with a Small Food Business*.

Other useful addresses
HMSO Publications
PO Box 276
London SW8 5DT
Tel: 071 873 9090
Can supply copies of the *Food Safety Act* 1990.

Farm Shop and Pick-Your-Own Association,
22 Long Acre
London WC2E 9LY
Tel: 071 235 5077

National Federation of Women's Institutes
104 New Kings Road
London SW6 4LY
Tel: 071 371 9300

Useful publication
Running Your Own Catering Company, by Judy Ridgway, published by Kogan Page.

Section four: business ideas

Typing
The Society of Authors
84 Drayton Gardens
London SW10 9SB
Tel: 071 373 6642

The Writers' Guild of Great Britain
430 Edgware Road
London W2 1EH
Tel: 071 723 8074

Computers
The Training Agency
Moorfoot
Sheffield S1 4PQ
Tel: 0742 753275
can give information on training in a number of skills including computers.

Translating
The Institute of Linguists
24a Highbury Grove
London N5 2EA
Tel: 071 359 7445

Translators' Association
84 Drayton Gardens
London SW10 9SB
Tel: 071 373 6642

Networking
The Department of Trade and Industry has a leaflet on how to tell the difference between reputable and cowboy firms. For a copy, phone 071 215 3342.

The Direct Selling Association (Tel: 071 497 1234) will tell you about their code of conduct.

On The level, is a beginner's guide to networking, published by PCI. For details, phone: 0379 740573.

Indexing
Society of Indexers
38 Rochester Road
London NW1 9JJ
Tel: 071 916 7809

Market research
The Market Research Society
15 Northburgh Street
London EC1V 0AH
Tel: 071 490 4911

Running an agency
The Employment Agencies Licensing Office
Department of Trade and Industry
EALO Exchange House
60 Exchange Road
Watford WD1 7HH
will give you details of your regional agency licensing office.

Writing
See Typing, above

Arvon Foundation
Totleigh Barton,
Sheepwash, Beaworthy
Devon EX21 5NS
Tel: 040 923 338

National Union of Journalists
314 Gray's Inn Road
London WC1X 8DP
Tel: 071 278 7916

Mills & Boon (Publishers) Ltd
Eton House
18–24 Paradise Road
Richmond
Surrey TW9 1SR
Tel: 081 948 0444

The *Writers' and Artists' Yearbook* is published by A & C Black.

Useful publications
The Post Office has a useful leaflet *How to send things you value through the post.*

Secrets of Successful Telephone Selling by Chris de Winter, published by Heinemann, £8.95

Section five: arts and crafts

Découpage
Hawkin & Co
St Margaret
Harleston
Norfolk IP20 0PJ
Tel: 0986 82482
Stock scraps for découpage.

Papier Mâché
The Art and Craft of Papier Mâché by Juliet Bawden, published by Mitchell Beazley
Papier Mâché by Susanne Haines, published by Letts.

Dressmaking
R.D. Franks Ltd
Market Place
Oxford Circus
London W1 8EJ
Tel: 071 636 1244
Have a catalogue of books, equipment for the fashion industry.

Toys
HMSO Leaflet SI 1974 No. 1367 gives you information on the *Toys (Safety) Regulations Act.*

Pottery
The Craftsmen Potters' Association
William Blake House
Marshall Street
London W1V 1LP
Tel: 071 437 7605

publishes a bi-monthly magazine, *Ceramic Review*. Books on pottery and tools can be bought from their shop at the above address.

Potterycrafts Ltd
Campbell Road
Stoke-on-Trent ST4 4ET
Tel: 0782 745000
has an illustrated catalogue of supplies and equipment, also a useful publication *The Potter's Handbook*.

Furniture restoration
Ask for *The Art and Antique Restorer's Handbook* by George Savage, published by Barrie & Rockliff, 1967, at your library.

Art restoration
Ask your library to get you *Art Restoration* by Francis Kelly, published by David & Charles, 1971.

Decorating glass
The Guild of Glass Engravers
8 Rathcoole Avenue
London N8 9NA
Tel: 081 348 8772
has a useful leaflet, *Starting from Scratch*, and has both beginner and craft members.

Painted Furniture
Paint Magic and *Paintability* by Jocasta Innes, published by Weidenfeld and Nicolson.

Section six: green-finger ideas

Unusual seeds
Thompson & Morgan
London Road, Ipswich
Suffolk IP8 3BU
Tel: 0473 688588

Chiltern Seeds
Boretree Style
Ulverston
Cumbria LA12 7PB
Tel: 0229 581137

Suffolk Herbs
Monks Farm
Pantlings Lane
Kelvedon
Essex CO5 9PG
Tel: 0376 572456

General
English Vineyard Association
38 West Park
London SE9 4RH
Tel: 081 857 0452

National Gardens Scheme
Hatchlands Park
East Plondon
Guildford GU4 7RT
Tel: 0483 211 535

Ministry of Agriculture, Fisheries and Food (MAFF)
3 Whitehall Place
London SW1A 2HH
Tel: 071 270 8080

Royal Horticultural Society
80 Vincent Square
London SW1P 2PB
Tel: 071 834 4333

Useful Publications

The Complete Book of Pressed Flowers, The Book of Potpourri by Penny Black, published by Dorling Kindersley.

Pressing and drying flowers: Microwave Craft Magic by Marjie Lambert, published by Apple Press.

Flower Drying with a Microwave by Titia Joosten, published by Sterling/Lark.

Growing Herbs by Rosemary Titterington, published by Crowood Press (how to run a herb farm).

Section seven: working with people and animals

Beauty

The International Health and Beauty Council
109 Felpham Road
Felpham
West Sussex PO322 7PW
Tel: 0243 842064
has a leaflet: *So You Want to be a Beauty Therapist.*

Language students

ARELS (Association for Recognised English Language Teaching Establishments in Britain)
2 Pontypool Place
Valentine Place
London SE1 8QF
Tel: 071 242 3136
Has a useful leaflet called *A foreign Student in Your Home,* and will advise on training courses.

Keep fit

The Keep Fit Association
Francis House
Francis Street
London SW1P 1DE
can advise on courses.

Colour consultant
Contact Color Me Beautiful, at
Freepost London SW8 3NS
Tel: 071 627 5211
The Color Me Beautiful books are published by Judy Piatkus
(Publishers) Limited, 5 Windmill Street, London W1P 1HF.

Children
National Childminding Association,
8 Masons Hill
Bromley
Kent BR2 9EY
Tel: 081 464 6164
produces a magazine and has useful leaflets such as *So you want
to be a childminder* and *How to survive as a childminder*.

The Pre-school Playgroups Association
61–63 King's Cross Road
London WC1X 9LL
Tel: 071 833 0991
has literature on how to start a playgroup.

The British Association for Early Childhood Education
111 City View House
463 Bethnal Green Road
London E2 9QH
Tel: 071 739 7594
gives advice on how to set up and run a nursery school.

Home Nursing
Both the Red Cross and the St John's Ambulance Brigade run
courses in home nursing. Contact your local branch.

Teaching
Music:
The Incorporated Society of Musicians
10 Stratford Place
London W1N 9AE
Tel: 071 629 4413
is worth joining if you have the qualifications to do so.

Teachers/Tutoring:
The Council for the Accreditation of Correspondence Colleges
27 Marylebone Road
London NW1 5JS
Tel: 071 935 5391
can send lists of colleges to apply to for work on correspondence courses.

Animals
The Royal Society for the Prevention of Cruelty to Animals
Causeway
Horsham
Sussex RH12 1HG
London Tel: 081 653 3420

Under *The Animal Establishments Act*, 1963, you must have a licence if you board animals on a large scale. Apply to your local authority.

Special insurance for pets, endorsed by the Kennel Club:

Pet Protect
55 High Street
Epsom
Surrey KT19 8DH
Tel: 0372 743472

Dog obedience, dog agility
The Kennel Club
1 Clarges Street
London W1Y 8AB
Tel: 071 629 5828

Poultry keeping
The *Slaughter of Poultry Act* and the *Animal Health and Welfare Act*, available from HMSO (address on page 191), sets out the permitted ways of killing birds.

The Domestic Fowl Trust
Honeybourne Pastures
Honeybourne
Evesham
Worcs WR11 5QJ
Tel: 0386 833083

Goat keeping
The Goat Advisory Bureau
Water Farm
Stogursey
Bridgwater
Somerset TA15 1PF
Tel: 0278 732 397

Further Reading:
Commercial Goat Keeping by Katie Thear, published by New
Leys Publishing Co.
A free leaflet, *Dairy Goat Keeping* is available from
The Ministry of Agriculture, Fisheries and Food Publications,
London SE99 7TP
Tel: 081 694 8862

Bee-keeping
Ministry of Agriculture, Fisheries and Food Publications (see
address above) have advisory leaflets on bee-keeping including,
Advice to intending Bee-keepers.

The British Bee-keepers Association
c/o the National Agricultural Centre
Stoneleigh
Kenilworth
Warwicks CV8 2LZ
Tel: 0203 696679
has a free leaflet, *Would you like to keep bees?*

The Agricultural Development & Advisory Service (ADAS) has
an apiary section at:

Luddington Experimental Horticultural Station
Stratford-on-Avon
Warwicks CV37 9SJ
who will give advice and answer queries.

Further reading:
The Beekeeper's Manual by Stephens-Potter, published by David & Charles.

General
City and Guilds run certificate courses in a wide range of practical subjects from running a guesthouse to a beauty salon.
City & Guilds of London Institute
76 Portland Place
London W1N 4AA
Tel: 071 278 2468

INDEX

accommodation addresses, 75
accountants, 74, 180
activity groups, children, 161
additives, food, 64
agencies, 90–1
  animal model, 173–4
  literary, 94–5
agility classes, dogs, 172–3
angora goats, 177
animals:
  agility training, 172–3
  beauty care, 171–2
  breeding, 169–70
  convalescent, 168
  dog obedience classes, 172
  goat keeping, 176–7
  kennels and catteries, 168–9
  model agencies, 173–4
  pet-sitting, 167–8
  poultry, 176
  quarantine, 170–1
  toys and accessories, 122–3
  working with, 166–77
  your own, 25
answering machines, 24
antiques, 91–2
appliqué, 107–8
art restoration, 128–9
artificial flowers, 131
arts and crafts, 102–33
astrology, 101

baking, 61–2
ballroom dancing, 166
bank loans, 186–8
basketry, 103–4
bathrooms, 35
batik, 108–9
BBC, 96
bean bags, 123
beauty business, 155–8, 175–6
bed and breakfast, 34, 40–3
bed-sitters, 35–7, 39
bee-keeping, 174–6
beeswax, 175
bio-rhythms, 101
birthday party catering, 67–8
biscuits, 61
blinds, 115
bookbinding, 125–6
book-keeping, 75
books:
  children's, 96–7
  cook books, 68–70
  fiction, 94–6
  handbooks, 132
breads, 61
breeding pets, 169–70
business ideas, 74–101
business plans, 187–8
business rates, 21
bye-laws, 21

cakes, 61, 62, 66–7
calligraphy, 130
cameras, 100
candle-making, 130–1
cane work, 103–4
capital, raising, 185–9
car boot sales, 140
cars:
 insurance, 182
 transporting food in, 73
cash and carry stores, 54
catering, 58–61, 65–8
 see also cookery
cats:
 breeding, 169–70
 cat-sitting, 168
 catteries, 168–9
 toys and accessories, 122–3
ceramics, 119–20
chairs, re-caning, 103–4
charity days, garden opening,
  140
cheese, goat's, 177
chickens, 176
children, 23–4
 activity groups, 161
 child-minding, 159–61
 fostering, 161–2
 party catering, 67–8
 playgroups and nurseries,
  160
 working with, 158–62
 writing for, 96–7
china:
 hiring out, 70
 repairs, 125
chocolate, confectionery, 65
christenings, catering, 66
chutneys, 63–4
Citizens' Advice Bureau, 19,
  178, 188–9

clothes:
 dolls', 118
 dress hire, 87–8
 dressmaking, 110–13
 knitted, 116–17
 working, 28–9
clubs, catering for, 68
coaching school children, 166
'cold calling', 81, 84
colour consultancy, 158
companies, setting up, 183–4
Companies' House, 179, 184
Companies' Registration
  Office, 184
computers:
 computer services, 78–80
 teaching skills, 165
 typing services, 76
confectionery, 65
convalescent pets, 168
conversions, building work,
  36–7
cookery, 48–73
 baking, 61–2
 buying ingredients, 54
 catering, 58–61
 costing, 72
 dinner parties, 70–1
 equipment, 52–3
 food for photography and
  films, 68
 foreign food, 68
 hygiene regulations, 49–51
 insurance, 73
 party catering, 65–8
 preserves, pickles and
  chutneys, 63–4
 for restaurants, wine bars
  and pubs, 62–3
 selling, 57

sweets and confectionery, 65
teaching, 164
transport, 73
writing cook books, 68–70
cooking facilities, bed-sitters, 35–7
correspondence colleges, 166
cosmetics, 175–6
costing:
  cooking, 72
  dressmaking, 111–12
  hairdressing, 157
covenants, 18
crafts, 102–33
creative writing, 94–7
credit cards, 188
crystallised fruits, 65
curtains, 114
cushions, 115
cuttings, perennial plants, 138–9
CVs, 77

dancing, teaching, 165–6
dealing, pictures and antiques, 91–4
découpage, 104
deposits, letting rooms, 46
designing letterheads, 80
desk-top publishing, 78, 79
dinner parties, 58–60, 70–1
dogs:
  agility training, 172–3
  breeding, 169–70
  dog-sitting and dog-walking, 167
  grooming, 171–2
  kennels, 168–9
  obedience classes, 172
  toys and accessories, 122–3

dolls, 118
dolls' houses, 121–2
dress hire, 87–8
dressmaking, 110–13
dried flowers, 142–3
DSS, 34
ducks, 176
dyeing fabrics, 108–10

eggs, 176
elderly, working with, 162
embroidery, 117
Employer's Liability
    (Compulsory Insurance)
    Act, 182
English, teaching, 163–4
Enterprise Councils, 189
Environmental Health
    departments, 50
equipment:
  cooking, 52–3
  gardening, 152–3
  hiring out, 70, 86–8
expenses, tax relief, 180–1

families, 23–6
faxing services, 75–6
fiction, writing, 94–6
film scripts, 96
films, food for, 68
finances:
  costing dressmaking, 111–12
  costing food, 72
  costing hairdressing, 157
  raising cash, 185–9
  see also costing
fine art, 127–30
finger food, 60
fire insurance, 182
fitness training, 157–8

flats, 37, 38–9
flowers, 141–3
    artificial, 131
    dried, 142–3
    flower arranging, 143–4
    pressed, 143
food *see* cookery
food additives, 64
Food Safety Act (1990), 49
food styling, 68
foreign food, 68
fostering children, 161–2
framing pictures, 126
freezers, 53, 64
friends, borrowing money
    from, 188
fruit:
    crystallised, 65
    growing, 146
    preserves, pickles and
        chutneys, 63–4
fun cakes, 66–7
furniture:
    painted, 131
    re-caning chairs, 103–4
    restoration, 123–4
    upholstery, 124–5

garages, 28
garden services, 150–1
gardening, 51–2, 134–54
geese, 176
glassware:
    decoration, 129–30
    hiring out, 70
    repairs, 125
goats, 176–7
graphology, 101
Greater London Business
    Centre, 178

greenhouses, 136, 148, 152
grooming animals, 171–2

hairdressing, 156–7
handbooks, writing, 132
handicapped people, working
    with, 162
hats:
    hiring out, 88
    making, 113
herbs, 51–2, 64, 146–8
hire purchase, 188
hiring at home, 88
hiring out, 70, 86–8
historic houses, 42
homeless people, 34
honey, 175
houseplants, 148–9
housework, 25
hygiene regulations, 49–51

I Ching, 101
illustration, 128
income tax, 180–1
indexing, 77, 85–6
indoor plants, 148–9
industrial estates, 33–4
Inland Revenue, 180
insurance, 181–3
    catering, 73
    freezers, 53
    hiring at home, 88
    letting rooms, 46
    selling, 80–1
interpreters, 78
ironing, 90

jewellery, 120–1
journalism, 97–9

keep fit trainers, 157–8
kennels, 168–9

kitchens:
  bed-sitters, 35–7
  hygiene regulations, 49–50
  knitting, 116–17

labelling, food, 64
lampshades, 115–16
landlords, 30
languages:
  teaching, 78, 163
  translating, 77–8
laundry services, 90
lavatories, 25–6
letterheads, designing, 80
letters, writing for foreigners, 78
letting rooms, 31–46
letting the whole house, 47
limited companies, 183–4
Loan Guarantee Scheme, 187
loans, 186–9
local authorities, planning permission, 18–21, 30–1, 37, 155–6, 168, 172
lodgers, 31–5, 37, 39–40, 43–6
loose covers, 115, 125
lunch parties, 58–60

machine knitting, 116–17
magazines, journalism, 97–9
mail order plants, 139, 140–1
market research, 84–5
milk, goat's, 176, 177
miniature plants, 139, 148
model agencies, animals, 173–4
model making, 121
mohair, 177
money, raising, 185–9

mortgages, 18, 30
motivation, 26–8
mushrooms, 137
music, teaching, 165
mustards, herb, 64

names, trade, 179–80
National Insurance, 183
needlepoint, 117
neighbours, 20–1
networking, 81–3
newspapers, journalism, 97–9
novels, 94–6
nurseries, 160–1

obedience classes, dogs, 172
office services, 75–80
offices, supplying plants to, 151
organic vegetables, 144
outworking, 89
overdrafts, 186

painting, 127–8
  furniture, 131
  on silk, 110
papier mâché, 104–5
partnerships, 183
party catering, 65–8
party hire, 87
party selling, 83–4
patchwork, 107–8
patents, 185
pattern-cutting, 110–11
pay-phones, 46
paying guests, 39–40
perennial plants, 138–9
petit fours, 65
pets *see* animals

photography, 99–100
  animal model agencies,
    173–4
  food, 68
photostatting services, 75–6
pickles, 63–4
pictures:
  framing, 126
  paintings, 127–8
  selling, 91, 93–4
picture libraries, 100
planning permission, 18–21,
    30–1, 37, 156, 168, 172
plant sitting, 151
plants, 134–54, 175
playgroups, 158–9, 160–1
plays, writing, 96
portrait painting, 127–8
pot plants, 148–9
pot-pourri, 143
pottery, 119–20
poultry, 176
presentation, food, 57
preserves, 63–4
pressed flowers, 143
printers, computer, 80
printing fabrics, 108–10
proofreading, 70, 85–6
public liability insurance, 182
publishing, desk-top, 78, 79
pubs, cooking for, 62–3

quarantine, 170–1
quilting, 113–14
quilts, patchwork, 107–8

rag rugs, 106
redundancy, 9
references, lodgers, 46
remedial teaching, 166
rent, lodgers, 46

repairs:
  china and glass, 125
  clothes, 112–13
  jewellery, 120–1
restaurants, cooking for, 62–3
restoration:
  furniture, 123–4
  paintings, 128–9
retirement, 9
romantic fiction, 95
rugs, 106
runes, reading, 101
Rural Development
    Commission, 178

salad crops, 145
sandwiches, 60–1
scratching posts, 123
search services, 85
seeds, 138
selling, 80–4
  insurance, 80–1
  networking, 81–3
  party selling, 83–4
  telephone selling, 81, 84
sewing-machines, 111
silk, painting on, 110
silk screen printing, 109
smoking, lodgers, 44
soft furnishings, 114–16
soft toys, 117–18
solicitors, 74
structured days, 22
student lodgers, 32–3, 43,
    44–6
studios, photographic, 100
sweets and confectionery, 65

tarot cards, 101
tax, income, 180–1
teaching, 132–3, 162–6

telephones, 24
   lodgers, 45–6
   telephone answering, 78
   telephone selling, 84
tenants, 31–46
textile crafts, 105–18
theft, insurance, 182
tie and dye, 109–10
tools, gardening, 152–3
topiary, 149, 150–1
tourists, 34, 40–3
toys, 117–18, 121–3
trade marks, 184–5
trade names, 179–80
Training Councils, 189
translating, 77–8
transport, catering, 73
trapunto, 114
travel writing, 98–9
tutoring, 166
typing, 76–7

upholstery, 124–5

VAT returns, 75
vegetables:
   growing, 144–6

preserves, pickles and
   chutneys, 63–4
venture capital, 188
vinegars, herb, 64
vineyards, 149–50

washing, 90
weaving, 105–7
weddings:
   catering, 66
   photographs, 99
   wedding dresses, 112
wine bars, cooking for, 62–3
wine making, 149–50
Women's Institute markets,
   62, 72
word processors, 76, 79–80
work rhythms, 21–2
workplaces, 27–8
writing:
   for children, 96–7
   cook books, 68–70
   fiction, 94–6
   handbooks, 132
   journalism, 97–9
   plays and film scripts, 96